Someone to trust – a nice environment, homely, that will raise their confidence. Toys and games to occupy their time. Someone to talk to them about what they are feeling and to help them to understand why it is better that they have left... You need people to understand how you are feeling and help you to cope with the changes.
(Boy, aged 15, who has experienced domestic violence at home, quoted in Mullender and others, 2002: 102)

People to listen to what you are saying and understand you more.
(Young person who has experienced parental substance misuse, quoted in Liverpool Drug and Alcohol Action Team, 2001: 21)

I think they should try to understand and listen, because if someone has listened to you and hasn't depersonalised you, have actually looked you in the eye and listened to you, then you feel a whole lot better.
(Girl, aged 17, who has lived with a parent with health problems, quoted in Newton and Becker, 1996: 33)

Understanding what children say

Children's experiences of domestic violence, parental substance misuse and parental health problems

Sarah Gorin

national children's bureau

00000312

Joseph Rowntree Foundation

The Joseph Rowntree Foundation has supported this project as part of its programme of research and innovative development projects, which it hopes will be of value to policy makers, practitioners and service users.

National Children's Bureau

The National Children's Bureau promotes the interests and well-being of all children and young people across every aspect of their lives. NCB advocates the participation of children and young people in all matters affecting them. NCB challenges disadvantage in childhood.

NCB achieves its mission by

- ensuring the views of children and young people are listened to and taken into account at all times
- playing an active role in policy development and advocacy
- undertaking high quality research and work from an evidence based perspective
- promoting multidisciplinary, cross-agency partnerships
- identifying, developing and promoting good practice
- disseminating information to professionals, policy makers, parents and children and young people

NCB has adopted and works within the UN Convention on the Rights of the Child.

Cruelty to children must stop. FULL STOP.

The National Society for the Prevention of Cruelty to Children (NSPCC, registered charity number 216401) is the UK's leading charity specialising in child protection and the prevention of cruelty to children. The NSPCC's purpose is to end cruelty to children. Its vision is of a society where all children are loved, valued and able to fulfil their potential. The Society seeks to achieve cultural, social and political change – influencing legislation, policy, practice, attitudes and behaviours for the benefit of children and young people. Sarah Gorin is a Senior Research Officer at the NSPCC and was funded by the Joseph Rowntree Foundation to undertake this review.

Published by the National Children's Bureau for the Joseph Rowntree Foundation.

National Children's Bureau, 8 Wakley Street, London EC1V 7QE. Tel: 020 7843 6000. Book Sales: 0845 458 9910. Website: www.ncb.org.uk
Registered Charity number 258825

© NSPCC 2004
Published 2004
Reprinted 2007

The views expressed in this book are those of the author and not necessarily those of the National Children's Bureau, the Joseph Rowntree Foundation, or NSPCC.

ISBN 1 904787 12 6

British Library Cataloguing in Publication Data
A catalogue record for this book is available from the British Library

Contents

Acknowledgements

We would like to acknowledge the Joseph Rowntree Foundation for funding the literature review under the Understanding Children's Lives Initiative and particular thanks to Susan Taylor for her support. The help and advice of Pat Cawson, Andrea Cornelius and Lucy Thorpe at the NSPCC is much appreciated. Thank you also to Audrey Mullender, Richard Olsen, Lorna Templeton, Neil McKeganey, Helen Evans and Jo Aldridge who kindly commented on drafts of the report.

1. Introduction

Background

This literature review examines what children say about living in families where there is domestic violence, parental substance misuse or parental health problems. The review was written to improve our understanding of how children experience these problems at home, how they cope with them and what support they need. In order to do this, the review draws largely on children's own direct accounts, as research suggests that children may have a very different outlook and preoccupations to those of adults (Hester and others, 1998; McGee, 2000; Aldgate and Statham, 2001). The review does not describe the experiences and needs of parents and other family members, although clearly meeting their needs is also important and may go a long way to helping children. The review should be read in conjunction with other literature published in each of these fields that reflects upon the experiences of other family members (for example, see Hester and others, 1998; Bates and others, 1999; Cleaver and others, 1999; Parton and Wattam, 1999; Harbin and Murphy, 2000; Humphreys and Mullender, 2000; Humphreys, 2001; Banks and others, 2002; Tunnard, 2002a, 2002b; Kroll and Taylor, 2003).

The experiences of parents and children will vary greatly both within and between each type of adversity discussed in the review. Many children, at some point in their childhood, will have parents who experience domestic violence, parental substance misuse or parental ill health. It is important to stress that these problems may not necessarily affect parenting capacity, nor should it be assumed that all of these parental problems will have a negative impact on children, either in the short or the long term. The review that follows is primarily concerned with understanding the experiences of children who are more vulnerable as a result of chronic or multiple problems at home and therefore may benefit from additional support. Among the children known to social services, domestic violence, parental substance misuse (drugs and alcohol) and parental health problems (physical and mental) are the most frequently cited family (rather than child or community) related factors that make children more vulnerable to poor outcomes (Department of Health, 1995; Falkov, 1996; Brandon and others, 1999; Corby, 2000; Aldgate and Statham, 2001).

The reason for looking across children's experiences of domestic violence, parental substance misuse and parental health problems is that despite the often very different circumstances of children, children who do experience chronic problems at home have a limited range of coping strategies available to them. There are also common messages about the support they value. Children themselves are unlikely to see their own lives in terms of one discrete problem at home. For most families their situation will be complex and their experiences of domestic violence, parental substance misuse or parental ill health will be part of a larger picture of disadvantage and/or stress in the family. Previous research carried out directly with children has tended to focus on one form of parental adversity and has tended to include children who live outside the home, rather than those living within the community (Barnard and Barlow, 2003).

The review is not concerned with causation or attributing blame for problems in the home and this is rarely a preoccupation of children. Nor does it wish to perpetuate myths about parents who experience domestic violence, substance misuse or ill health as being 'poor parents'. Indeed, it is recognised that the stigma attached to parental problems can perpetuate difficulties for children and families in seeking and getting the help that they need (Houston and others, 1997). However, it is important to highlight these children's experiences because the complex dynamics that may surround these families mean that it can be difficult for parents and professionals to get a sense of the feelings children may be experiencing and the support they might value.

Policy and practice context

In order to understand these children's experiences and needs, it is helpful to review where they fit into the current policy and practice framework. Recognition of the particular vulnerability of these children and of the possible impact on their well-being is slowly increasing. For example, the Emerging Findings of the National Service Framework (NSF) for Children recognises that children with 'troubled parents for example children of substance misusing parents, children living with domestic violence, children whose parents have mental health problems, children with parents in prison and young carers' require specific attention, as they may often experience poorer outcomes than their peers (Department of Health, 2003a). In the field of domestic violence there has also been a step forward in terms of policy. The definition of 'harm' in section 31 subsection (9) of the Children Act, (1989) has been amended by section 120 of the Children and Adoption Act (2002) to include 'impairment suffered from seeing or hearing the ill-treatment of another'. The needs of children of problem drug users have also been highlighted by a report by the Home Office Advisory Council on the Misuse of Drugs (ACMD) (2003). This makes 48 recommendations for improvements to professional practice and service provision. These include the recommendation that 'the voices of children of problem drug users should be heard and listened to' and that 'work is required to develop means of enabling the children of problem drug users safely to express their thoughts and feelings about their circumstances' (p.11). However, few policy documents reflect the extent of the problems and the possible impact on children. For example, the report by the ACMD (2003), remarks that although the Updated Drug Strategy (Drug Strategy Directorate, 2002) does provide some references to children of problem drug users, the 'lack of attention…is an indication that at a strategic level, neither the number of children involved nor the extent of their needs has yet been fully recognised' (p.64).

Although awareness about the possible impact of parental problems on children is slowly increasing in policy, this recognition has not been accompanied by a level of resources adequate to develop service provision to meet their needs. Services in the fields of domestic violence, parental substance misuse and parental health problems have been traditionally focused on meeting the needs of the parent with the recognition that this may also consequently improve outcomes for the child. Focusing on supporting adults may mean that children's needs remain invisible. The concept of providing services that holistically address the needs of all family members when a parent has experienced domestic violence, parental substance misuse or parental health problems is relatively new. Only a small number of services exist and these are largely provided by the voluntary sector. Although the statutory sector provides some funding for services such as women's refuges, these are often unable to meet the needs of all mothers and children who would benefit from such a service. Similarly, there are only a very limited number of places available for mothers to take their children and attend residential drug and alcohol rehabilitation services. Childcare during treatment is a significant problem for many parents. Despite it often being a struggle to gain or maintain secure funding for such projects, there are examples of exceptional services providing support to families and children where there is domestic violence or parental drug/alcohol misuse (Hague and others, 1996; ACMD, 2003; Templeton and others, 2003).

In some cases where services specifically for children do exist, access may not always be straightforward. The process of assessment and service entitlement for 'young carers' (children whose parents have health or substance misuse problems and who provide a substantial amount of care on a regular basis) can be complex (for further information see Aldridge and Becker, 2003).

How many children experience these problems at home?

No exact figures are available about how many children live in families where there is domestic violence, parental substance misuse and parental ill health. The figures that exist generally show a wide variation in estimates depending on the methods and the definitions employed by researchers. The closest estimates are likely to be based on census information or prevalence surveys that are extrapolated onto the general population. Both of these are reliant on parents self-reporting so are likely to be vast underestimates, as many families conceal problems.

Estimates of the number of children whose parents have problematic alcohol use vary but are around 1 million and above. The Prime Minister's Strategy Unit has published the Alcohol Harm Reduction Strategy for England. It suggests that up to 1.3 million children are affected by parental alcohol problems (Prime Minister's Strategy Unit, 2004). Orford (2001) bases an estimate on 2 to 3 million adults being 'alcohol dependent', and therefore suggests that the number of children affected could be as many as 4 to 6 million.

Drug misuse affects a smaller but not insignificant number of children. The report by the ACMD (2003) estimated that there are between 200,000 and 300,000 children (under 16 years old) of problem drug users in England and Wales, and between 40,800 to 58,700 in Scotland. The proportion of children with parents who have problem drug use in England and Wales is estimated to be between 2 and 3 per cent; and in Scotland it is estimated as being between 4 and 6 per cent (ACMD 2003). These figures are based on self-reporting by parents and on parents who have attended treatment, therefore are likely to underestimate the prevalence in the general population.

In the first national prevalence study in the UK using a random probability general population sample of 2,869 young adults (aged 18–24 years old), more than 26 per cent had witnessed violence between parents at least once and for 5 per cent this was a constant or frequent occurrence (Cawson and others, 2000). A report by the Department of Health (2003b) estimates that at least 750,000 children a year witness domestic violence and three-quarters of the children on the Child Protection Register (CPR) live in households where domestic violence occurs.

Cawson and others (2000) also found that 14 per cent of young people had to assume adult responsibilities in childhood because parents were ill, disabled, had personal problems, substance misuse or left children unsupervised regularly.

The Green Paper *Every Child Matters* estimates that there are around 150,000 'young carers', a significant number of whom provide many hours of care every week (Department for Education and Skills (DfES), 2003a).

Another source of information often quoted is from official statistics, however these only represent the number of children/families or incidents presenting to services. Information from families in contact with Social Service Departments suggests a much higher level of problems of domestic violence, parental substance misuse and parental ill health than in the general population. These figures disproportionately represent families that experience poverty, social disadvantage and exclusion and are less likely to identify children living in more affluent families, those that move frequently, are homeless, adolescents and others who remain invisible to the system.

As at 31 March 2003, there were 26,600 children on the Child Protection Register (CPR) in England. Of these, 40 per cent of children were registered in the category of neglect, 16 per cent for physical abuse, 19 per cent for emotional abuse, 10 per cent for sexual abuse and 15 per cent in mixed categories (DfES, 2003b). A study undertaken in four London local authorities has found that drugs and alcohol affected more than a third of all cases dealt with by social services. Forty per cent of children on the CPR and 62 per cent of those cases subject to care proceedings involved parental substance misuse. Alcohol misuse was found to be the most frequently used substance (Forrester, 2002). Another study in one inner London local authority found that of the families of children on the CPR over a six month period, 65 per cent were experiencing or had experienced domestic violence, 63 per cent had substance misuse problems (drugs or alcohol misuse), 57 per cent had mental health problems and 33 per cent had health problems (Gorin, forthcoming). Estimated prevalence of parental mental health problems, parental substance misuse and domestic violence have been shown to increase as child welfare concerns become more serious and many of these concerns are associated with more intractable cases (Cleaver and others, 1999; Forrester, 2002).

In families where there is more than one problem, children are more vulnerable, particularly where violence between parents is combined with parental substance misuse, children witness violence between parents, are drawn into violence towards a parent or into maintaining secrecy about violence (Cleaver and others, 1999). Violence between parents has also been highlighted as a predictor of violence towards children (Farmer and Owen, 1995; Cawson, 2002). However, little is known about the number of families that exist where there are multiple problems. In the research by Gorin (forthcoming), it was found that in the majority of children's lives who were on the CPR (104 children out of 136) there were two or more of the following five family factors present: domestic violence, drug misuse, alcohol misuse, physical or mental health problems.

How might children be affected?

Having a positive experience of family life is important for all children and is likely to increase their chances of having a healthy development and transition to adulthood. There is now more recognition that if parents are having chronic problems this is likely to impact on their children, particularly if they are also living within the home (Cleaver and others, 1999; Cowling, 1999; Velleman and Orford, 1999; Hogan and Higgins, 2001). However the extent to which living with a parent who experiences difficulties impacts upon the child is extremely variable and dependent on a whole range of factors, not least the specific nature and extent of parental problems. For many families, particularly where one problem exists in isolation, children's experiences and their life chances may be no worse than for any other child growing up in similar socio-economic circumstances (Laybourn and others, 1996; Velleman and Orford, 1999; Newman, 2002).

In families that are experiencing domestic violence, parental substance misuse and parental health problems, there are often multiple stressors that can compound problems for parents and may affect parenting capacity and impact on children. These stressors include poverty, poor housing, homelessness, long-term unemployment, inequality, racism and other forms of social exclusion and discrimination (Dearden and Becker, 2000; Aldgate and Statham, 2001). Other factors that may also affect outcomes for children include relationship conflict, chaotic lifestyles, problematic parenting and children's increased responsibility in the home. Family disharmony has been found to be a significant indicator of increased risk to outcomes for children when combined with parental mental health problems or substance misuse (Velleman and Orford, 1999; Cleaver and others, 1999). Provision of support (informal and formal) to children and families may help them to overcome some of the difficulties they experience.

A literature review by Cleaver and others (1999) outlines the research evidence about the ways in which domestic violence, parental substance misuse and parental mental health may impact upon children at different stages in their physical and emotional development. Some of the problems children may experience include physical injury; physical or emotional neglect; feelings of fear, sadness, anger, anxiety, guilt, concern for their parents, low self-esteem; bed wetting, sleep and eating problems, aggressive behaviour, withdrawal; running away; problems at school or in developing peer relationships; social isolation; inappropriate caring responsibilities for their age; exposure to drugs or paraphernalia (for example needles) or involvement/exposure to criminal activity.

Children who experience domestic violence, parental substance misuse or parental ill health whilst they are growing up may be at increased risk of problems in the long term (Cleaver and others, 1999). A recent Barnardo's report suggests that witnessing or experiencing violence could have long lasting emotional effects on children into adulthood, affecting ability to create and maintain relationships, self-esteem, self-confidence and stability, education and career prospects (Webster and others, 2002). As yet there are no full-scale longitudinal studies in the UK of children who grow up in families where there are these problems. Retrospective studies with adults who have grown up in families where there is parental substance misuse or parental health problems show that they may experience problems into adulthood (for example, Velleman and Orford, 1999; Dearden and Becker, 2000). It is difficult to say to what extent these experiences are a result of parental problems during childhood rather than of any other contributory factors, however some studies such as Velleman and Orford (1999) have tried to clarify this by using control groups. Children who have provided a significant amount of care to parents whilst they were growing up and whose education has been disrupted are thought to be more vulnerable to unemployment in adulthood and associated disadvantages such as poverty, poor housing and isolation. Children whose parents have drug and alcohol problems may also be more vulnerable themselves to developing mental health problems and misusing substances (Velleman, 1993; Hogan, 1998; Scottish Executive, 2001; McKeganey and others, 2002).

Definitions

For the purpose of the review the following definitions will be used.

- Domestic violence will be defined as 'Any violence between current and former partners in an intimate relationship, wherever or whenever the violence occurs.

The violence may include physical, sexual, emotional and financial abuse. Domestic violence occurs across society, regardless of age, gender, race, sexuality, wealth and geography. However, it is predominantly women who suffer as a result of it.' (Home Office, 2003)

■ The term 'substance' is used because it encompasses all drugs, both illicit drugs (such as heroin and other opiates, benzodiazepines, cocaine or amphetamines) and non-illicit drugs (such as alcohol and prescribed drugs and solvents). 'Misuse' is used because it implies harm and refers to the use of substances as part of problematic or harmful behaviour.

■ 'Parents with health problems (physical and mental)' includes any parent who is disabled or has chronic or recurring serious physical or mental health problems.

■ Children are defined as all those under the age of 18.

■ 'Parents' are defined broadly so as to include all those that may take parental responsibility for children, including step-parents/partners of parents, foster/adoptive parents, grandparents and so on.

The decision to include children's experiences of parental physical health problems in the review was not straightforward. Parenting capacity is clearly not affected in many families in which parents have a physical illness or disability. However, there are families in which parental physical health problems may directly or indirectly cause difficulties for children, particularly if physical illness is combined with other problems such as domestic violence, substance misuse, or mental ill health. Studies of family support services and of parents living in poor environments show that those who use these services or who have higher levels of need often also experience proportionally high levels of physical health problems (Thoburn and others, 2000; Ghate and Hazel, 2002; Gardner, 2003). It is often not clear whether poverty leads to poor health or the reverse. Another reason for inclusion of parental health problems is that many studies (particularly of 'young carers') do not distinguish between those children whose parents have physical or mental health problems.

Methods

The review examines completed and ongoing research undertaken in the UK within the broader context of international literature. The main emphasis, however, is on UK research. It covers relevant research from 1990 until early 2003.

Information about children's experiences of domestic violence, parental substance misuse and parental ill health comes from three main sources, that is, research that has asked:

- children directly about their experiences
- young adults about their own childhood experiences
- parents about their perceptions of children's experiences.

The review focuses primarily on research that has been undertaken directly with children about their experiences. This is supplemented with research from retrospective accounts by young adults who have grown up in families with these problems and from parents who have been asked about their children's experiences. These retrospective accounts were limited to studies that included accounts from young adults under the age of 35. It is not a comprehensive review of retrospective accounts or parent's accounts but it does draw upon them to enhance children's accounts by adding a different dimension that incorporates the possibility of adults' reflection in the context of longer life experiences.

Forty studies that included children's accounts or young adults' retrospective accounts about domestic violence, parental ill health and parental substance misuse were reviewed (see Appendix 3). A further six ongoing studies that are interviewing children were also found (see Appendix 4 for a summary). Approximately a further 50 related books and journal articles were also reviewed. See Appendix 1 for further details about the search strategy.

The focus of the review is children's experiences of parental problems *in the home*. The review does not examine research about children's views on living outside the home, for example what they think about being looked after by the local authority or living with relatives or friends. All the stresses that children may experience, at home, at school and in the community cannot be covered, but the review makes reference to research findings where they are of particular relevance. The choice of inclusion of problems does not mean that it is not recognised that many other difficulties may impact significantly upon the experience of the child and may be happening alongside experiences of the adversities that will be covered.

There are important limitations to the body of research with children and these should be borne in mind when reading the report. For a more detailed discussion see Appendix 2.

2. Understanding children's experiences

This chapter describes the key themes that arise in children's accounts of their experiences of living with domestic violence, parental substance misuse and parental ill health. These are discovery of parental problems, trying to understand parents' behaviour, violence and conflict, risk of maltreatment, responsibilities in the home, disruptions in education and difficulties making or maintaining friendships.

Children's discovery of parental problems

One of the most striking themes in the literature on children's experiences of domestic violence and parental substance misuse is the level of awareness children have about what is going on within their family. The literature on domestic violence shows that whilst the violence is ongoing, parents often underestimate how much children have seen, heard or understood (Jaffe and others, 1990). A detailed study by McGee (2000) of 54 children and 48 mothers who had experienced domestic violence, reports that after leaving the violent situation, mothers were shocked by how aware even their small children had been of the violence and how accurate their memories were. One mother said how it had even affected young babies.

> There was always an atmosphere, you know, you could cut it with
> a knife sometimes. Even as babies they can sense, sense it. 'Cause
> I always thought it was colic to be honest and I'm giving them
> Infacol and took 'em to the doctor's and the doctor's saying 'No
> there's nothing wrong with them'. And I thought, 'Well why the
> hell do they scream then, you know?' And they used to scream
> like they were in pain.
> *(McGee, 2000: 99)*

Once away from the violent situation mothers are more likely to find out the true extent of children's awareness. In a study by Abrahams (1994) with 108 mothers who had left violent situations, almost nine in ten said that they now thought that their children had been aware of the violence at home.

Similarly, in research on parental drug and alcohol misuse, parents are reported to try to conceal their habits and often believe they have been successful. Research by Barnard and Barlow (2003) interviewed 62 parents accessing inpatient and outpatient facilities for drug misuse (mainly heroin) and 36 of their children. They found that although most children could not pinpoint an age at which they became aware of the drug use, they knew far earlier and in much more detail about drug use than their parents thought to be the case. One child is reported as saying:

> I was seven, but she didnae know until I was about ten...My Ma's boyfriend brought all these people up to the house and that. But my Ma didnae want them in anyway. And they were taking stuff in the living room and all that...and I was going to the kitchen to get a drink and I seen my Ma taking something and then she didnae know that. And then sometimes I knew where she hid all her stuff when she was taking it and I'd go and I'd find them and all that but she didnae know. And then her meth, she said it was just medicine for her back and all that because she's got loads of like back troubles. But we knew that wisnae true either, we knew what it was for and all that and she only found out a wee while ago that we knew all that.
>
> *(Barnard and Barlow, 2003: 51)*

In Hogan and Higgins' study (2001) of 50 drug-using and 50 non-drug-using parents, parents were reported to try to conceal drug taking from children and maintained a strict taboo around talking about it. Younger children were more likely to witness drug taking because parents did not see it as damaging if it was at an age when they thought children could not understand. Parental desire to conceal drug misuse was also reported in interviews with 30 recovering heroin addicts in a study by McKeganey and others (2002). However, they similarly report that there were many occasions when children had witnessed drug use. In a study with 25 parents and 20 children, parents also reported trying to keep drug use hidden but it was not clear whether their motivation was to protect their children or through fear of further stigma or both (Liverpool Drug and Alcohol Action Team (DAAT), 2001). In Barnard and Barlow (2003) only two of the 62 parents who were interviewed had directly acknowledged that they had a drug problem to their children, and in these cases it was referred to in terms of an illness for which they needed medication.

Children's accounts show that the concealment of drug taking in the household can make children feel isolated or confused. Barnard and Barlow (2003) describe how a child aged 11 reported feeling angry because he thought that his father did not like him because he would not let him in the sitting room. Eventually his mother explained about the drug misuse in order to help him understand. This study also reports that several children only became aware of their parent's drug misuse through the taunts of other children.

The age at which children become aware of problems in the home or that other families are any different from their own varies (not least because problems may not start until the child is older). A Danish study on parental alcohol abuse with 20 families (32 children aged 5 to 16 years old) found that children started to understand what was going on at around the age of four or five (Christensen, 1997). Velleman and Orford's retrospective study (1999) with 164 adults who were children of problem drinkers found that children recalled becoming aware of parents' drinking when they were 3.5 years old. The mean age that young adults recalled definitely knowing about parents' drinking was 9.6 years.

Interestingly, literature about parental illness does not seem to cover children's discovery of problems in the same way. Most of the literature on children of parents with physical or mental health problems looks at 'young carers' and their roles, responsibilities and feelings, and within this it may also consider the onset of provision of care, but this does not necessarily coincide with the onset of their parent's problems. Children seem to be rarely asked about how they first found out about their parent's health problems and whether their feelings or understanding of the problems have changed over time.

Trying to understand parents' behaviour

Although children may be aware of problems at home, the research suggests that they do not always understand what is happening or why. Children's accounts of living with parents who have substance misuse problems describe a wide range of parental behaviours that they find difficult to understand. Young adults whose parents had a drinking problem in the study by Velleman and Orford (1999) reported remembering strange behaviour by parents; finding a parent or parents incapacitated; violence or rows between parents; parents not coming home or coming home late; accidents; parents hiding alcohol, sleeping more than normal or experiencing health problems. In a study by Laybourn and others (1996) with 20 children of parents with problematic alcohol misuse, children as young as five or six years old could describe the consequences of their parents' drinking.

> *Child:* Aha. She was sick.
> *Interviewer:* She was sick. Sometimes people have different kinds of sickness – do you know what kind of sickness it was?
> *Child:* Maybe she was…Aye! (with emphasis) I know how it is noo. 'Cause she was drinking too much beer.
> *(Laybourn and others, 1996: 45)*

Similarly, the 36 children in Barnard and Barlow (2003) reported witnessing a range of inconsistent behaviours by parents who had problem drug use, including being 'moanie', bad tempered, 'slow', 'sleepy', too busy to spend time with them and never having any money. Parents with problem drug use also report that children may see them taking drugs, see paraphernalia and have strangers coming into the household. In Hogan and Higgins (2001), 40 per cent of children of drug users were reported (by parents and professionals) to have witnessed drug taking and 44 per cent had seen drugs, drug taking equipment or 'works' in their homes. Children may also witness or get caught up in criminal behaviour, most often shoplifting (ACMD, 2003). In the study by McKeganey and others (2002) one parent says:

> My oldest boy was treble streetwise 'cos he was brought up that way. He'd been in the jail and things like that with us (visiting relatives) and I'd take him out (stealing) with me, get the jail and my mum would need to come to the police station and get him and things like that.
> *(McKeganey and others, 2002: 240)*

Helpline data shows that children also find violent or neglectful behaviour confusing and difficult to understand (Saunders with Epstein, Keep and Debbonaire, 1995; Houston and others, 1997; McGee, 2000). An in-depth study with 45 children that had lived with domestic violence shows that unless children had witnessed or knew about an explicitly violent incident, many were uncertain about what was going on or why (Mullender and others, 2002). One 13-year-old Asian boy said:

> I wasn't really sure what was going on at the time. I didn't really understand what was going on, but I know my mam and dad were fighting every day. I understand more now.
> *(Mullender and others, 2002: 94)*

Children who have a parent with mental health problem also report finding it hard to understand the parent's behaviour at times, especially if the nature of their illness means that they act in bizarre ways or put their own safety at risk. Shah and Hatton

(1999) in a study with 19 young people with caring responsibilities found that changes in parents' behaviour could be traumatic for children, especially if they were young. Elliot (1992) undertook a study with nine young people who provided care for parents with mental health problems. One young person said:

> From the age of six I never trusted her. She tried to jump out of
> the bathroom window and I held on to her until a neighbour
> came, I was very confused about why she wanted to do this.
> *(Elliot, 1992: 16)*

A study by Aldridge and Becker (2003) interviewed children of parents with a mental illness, on two occasions (40 children initially and 28 again at a later date). In this study, one child described her confusion at her mother's behaviour.

> Mummy likes to drink a lot and it doesn't mix with her medicine
> and her medicine don't mix with the, what she drinks and she'll
> forget what she's doing when she drinks and she like starts
> talking a lot and the next minute you know she's like speaking
> into another world and that's what gets me really confused when
> I don't understand what she's talking about. She'll start asking
> funny questions. She'll be sleeping on the floor, weeing and
> going to the toilet in the wrong place.
> *(Aldridge and Becker, 2003: 79)*

In a Canadian study by Garley and others (1997) with six children, one boy talked about struggling to make sense of his mother's moods.

> I could tell that she was sick or something…cause…she usually
> would get mad at me…or sometimes she'd cry or something.
> That was hard for me to understand 'cause I didn't know what
> she was crying about.
> *(Garley and others, 1997: 100)*

Despite some children finding behaviour confusing, studies have shown that children are often able to identify factors that led up to domestic violence, parental substance misuse or parental mental health problems. In Mullender and others (2002), children even of a young age showed an insight into the power and control behind the violence towards their mother. One child is reported as saying:

> When my mum went out [with her women friends on her
> birthday], I reckon Dad was jealous because Mum was having a
> good time and I don't think he liked it.
> *(Mullender and others, 2002: 185)*

Houston and others (1997) undertook an in-depth study of 2,134 records of children's calls to ChildLine that mentioned parental alcohol misuse and found that many of them could identify problems leading up to problem drinking usually associated with a stressful change in family circumstances.

Parental violence and conflict

Research on parental problems at home (excluding research on parental physical health problems alone) highlights the increased risk that children may experience violence towards themselves, witness or overhear violence to others or experience higher levels of relationship conflict (arguing, fighting and rows) between adults in the household. Alcohol misuse is often particularly associated with violent behaviour (ChildLine, 1995; Brisby and others, 1997; Velleman and Orford, 1999; Forrester, 2000). Alcohol may be an acute or chronic factor that results in domestic violence (Velleman, 1993), substance misuse may be used as a means of coping with domestic violence and it may also be used as an excuse for violent behaviour. The negative impact on children of witnessing domestic violence is well documented (Hester and others, 1998).

In Abrahams (1994) the most common experiences children had, were seeing their mother upset or crying, witnessing violence, being aware of the atmosphere at home, and overhearing attacks. Children in the studies of domestic violence give very frank accounts of witnessing brutal attacks.

> He tried to get her to drink the bleach, to pour it in her mouth whilst he held her there and when he couldn't make her, he poured bleach all over her face and hair. He was trying to kill her.
> *(Mullender and others, 2002: 94)*

Despite the awfulness of attacks such as these, some children report that they need to know what is happening to their mother during an assault because they fear the worst.

> Just tell me things and not shut the door so that I don't know (what's happening). He could have stuck a knife in her for all I know, with the door shut. And the worst thing for me was actually not knowing what was going to happen next, not knowing what was happening then and not knowing what was going to happen next. That was the most frightening thing for me.
> *(McGee, 2000: 107).*

Aldridge and Becker (2003) in their study of children caring for parents with mental illness found that in the few cases of violence towards children or where children were frightened by parents' behaviour in their sample, mental health problems coexisted with drug and alcohol misuse.

Children's fear of violence is often compounded by the uncertainty and unpredictability of a parent's moods and actions. Epstein and Keep analysed a random sample of 126 phone calls to ChildLine about domestic violence (Saunders with Epstein, Keep and Debbonaire, 1995). They report that in cases where a parent is violent children can feel like they are 'walking on egg shells', afraid that anything they might do may bring about a violent response. An evaluation of a pilot project to support children affected by domestic violence shows that children who live with a parent who is violent or verbally aggressive often become accustomed to an unpredictable world in which they never know when a parent might 'flip' and start shouting, swearing and breaking belongings (Wright, 2002). The following quote from Mullender and others (2002) supports this.

> It was the worst part of my life – constantly being shouted at,
> frightened, living in fear. You will never know what it's like,
> thinking that every day could be your last.
> *(Mullender and others, 2002: 94)*

As McGee (2000) points out, fear and unpredictability do not just exist when there is violence, children can also feel threatened when there is relationship conflict. Children who hear parents arguing constantly are likely to be concerned for their parent and the child may fear for the future.

> I can hear my parents arguing when I'm lying in bed at night.
> Sometimes they're arguing about me. I can't sleep and I can't
> stop worrying. Quite often I'm afraid to go down in the morning.
> *(Butler and Williamson, 1994: 55)*

A pilot research project by the Domestic Advice Line in Gloucestershire interviewed ten children, one of the children talked about how nervous they felt when their dad got angry.

> My dad's got a bad temper, he takes things out on everybody, not
> just my mum...I understand what he says but only after about six
> times because I forget and then he'll shout at me. He won't hit me
> but when he shouts at me it makes me cry because I'm very nervous.
> *(Domestic Violence Advice Line, 1997: 27)*

Velleman and Orford (1999) found young adults reported family disharmony to be of central importance to understanding parental problem-drinking. The findings suggest that if parental alcohol misuse leads to family disharmony the child is substantially more likely to have adjustment difficulties, but if drinking does not lead to disharmony then there may be no more risk than for the average child within the study's comparison group.

Risk of maltreatment

Some of the accounts from children whose parents experience domestic violence or substance misuse highlight the risk that they or their siblings may also experience maltreatment (abuse or neglect).

Physical abuse

Direct accounts from children, particularly in cases of domestic violence, frequently report physical abuse or witnessing of physical abuse towards siblings. One young adult in Hill and others (1996), reported very severe abuse by his father and stepmother when they were drunk and angry.

> I was tied to a chair, tied up by the wrists – that's how bad it was. You know that sheep-dip stuff, you know, poisonous stuff, I had that poured down my throat as well.
> *(Hill and others, 1996: 163)*

Mullender and others (2002) found that children who overheard or witnessed violence were the most likely to talk about threats or experience of abuse towards themselves or siblings.

> He used to say, 'I am going to kill you at night-time when you are all asleep'. He used to come with an axe and say 'I am going to kill you'. I used to get very frightened. We had a lock on the bedroom doors in case he did what he said. He made a hole with an axe through my sister's bedroom door. Then he used to look through the hole.
> *(Mullender and others, 2002: 94)*

Children whose parents have drug/alcohol problems in the study by Liverpool DAAT (2001) were very direct in their descriptions of violence and abuse when discussing an imaginary family where there were drug/alcohol problems. Caution should be taken in interpreting the comments children made, as they were not asked to describe their own experiences. Children in the study said:

> The dad might batter you.

> Dad shouts a lot. He hits mum and the kids.

> Dad would force children to take drugs.

> The mum makes the kids take drugs.
> *(Liverpool DAAT, 2001: 17)*

Emotional abuse

Emotional abuse is implicit in many of the cases described in the section above in which children witness domestic violence or are verbally threatened, frightened or intimidated. One child in the Laybourn and others (1996) study describes how, although their mother was the one physically hurt, they were emotionally hurt.

> *Child:* My mum was affected by getting hit and all that and we were affected inside.
> *Interviewer:* Are you saying your Mum got hit and it hurt?
> *Child:* Ma Mum got hurt on the outside and we got hurt on the inside.
> *(Laybourn and others, 1996: 163)*

In the study by Mullender and others (2002) an eight-year-old mixed-race boy explains how he still feels emotionally confused following domestic violence.

> My mum is better, but I'm not. Can I say a bit about it? You know, how it has made me feel? It affected me a lot. It gets me all muddled and weird…I think it has frozen me up a bit inside.
> *(Mullender and others, 2002: 111)*

Neglect and chaotic lifestyles

Parents that are experiencing problems may find it difficult to meet their children's physical and emotional needs. In many cases, problems in parenting may be intermittent and not significant enough to constitute any likely harm to children. However, in other cases, physical or emotional neglect may place children at risk of significant harm.

Physical neglect and absence of supervision is particularly reported in research on substance misuse where parents are absent from home acquiring drugs or drinking or undertaking criminal activity. Problems with meeting children's physical and emotional needs in the case of substance misuse is most likely to occur when parents are in the process of taking drugs or drinking, or experiencing the after-effects or withdrawal. In the study by Hogan and Higgins (2001) parents with substance misuse problems reported that the greatest threat to their capacity to care for children was when they were experiencing anxiety and sickness during withdrawal. Although this may not constitute neglect, it can lead to chaotic lifestyles and an absence of routines for children.

> Sometimes we are late for school and don't have any breakfast.
> *(Liverpool DAAT, 2001: 18)*

Even if parents are physically present, children may experience parents as being emotionally unavailable. Children and parents report that changes in mood caused by drugs can also mean that children do not know what to expect from parents and they may feel rejected. A drug-using mother of a seven-year-old girl said:

> They wouldn't know whether you were coming or going…they
> don't know if you'll come back happy, whether you'll be roaring
> or playing with them or sending them to watch TV.
> *(Hogan and Higgins, 2001: 11)*

Similarly, short cycles of changing moods associated with alcohol misuse may mean that parents are happy and loving then withdrawn or violent and aggressive within a short period of time (Brisby and others, 1997).

All the parents in the study by Liverpool DAAT (2001) reported being aware that their need for drugs and alcohol could take priority over their children's needs. Children in the study by Barnard and Barlow (2003) report feeling that parents were not 'there for them' in the ways that they needed them to be.

> *Interviewer:* Did you feel that your parents were [there] for you
> that time? I mean that they were interested in you?
> *Respondent:* No. I knew they loved me but they just didnae care
> that I was there and I needed stuff as well. And I need this and
> things and they were just away taking drugs and stuff.
> *(Barnard and Barlow, 2003: 53)*

Sexual abuse

There is very little in children's direct accounts of domestic violence and parental substance misuse about experiences of sexual abuse. However as sexual abuse is the most likely form of abuse to be hidden, and studies may not ask children directly about abuse, its prevalence is likely to be underestimated. In McGee's (2000) research with 54 children who had experienced domestic violence, six children volunteered information about sexual abuse. In three cases, the violent man was the father and in the other three cases it was the stepfather. One of the children, a 15-year-old girl talks in the research about how the sexual abuse was combined with emotional abuse which made it harder to disclose information about the sexual abuse.

> He used to touch me like when I was in bed. He used to always
> sort of sit us down and go on about how we didn't love him and
> things and he was going to die and stuff like that.
> *(McGee, 2000: 56)*

Another child also reported that the perpetrator used threats towards her mother to try to silence her. All the children in McGee's study who had been sexually abused were aware of the violence to their mothers and so understood what the violent man was capable of.

Responsibilities in the home

A key theme that runs throughout the literature on children's experiences of domestic violence, parental substance misuse and parental ill health is about the increase in support that children may provide to parents who are going through difficulties. 'Young carers' have largely been seen as children whose parents have physical and mental health problems or substance misuse problems. However, children whose mothers have experienced domestic violence also provide accounts of supporting them emotionally and physically, sometimes by acting to protect them.

There are a number of studies on children with caring responsibilities. These include Grimshaw (1991), Aldridge and Becker (1993, 2003), Frank and others (1999), Dearden and Becker (1995, 1996, 1998, 2000), Newton and Becker (1996) and Walker (1996) among others. These have all documented the types of tasks children may undertake in the home to help support parents. These include domestic tasks (for example cooking, housework, shopping, gardening, budgeting), general care tasks (for example lifting or helping a parent to move, helping them take medication), intimate care tasks (for example helping a parent to dress, wash, go to the toilet), emotional support (dealing with distress or depression, building confidence or discussing problems) and care for siblings (supervision, taking children to school).

Banks and others (2001), found that the level of support that children may provide is likely to depend on the nature of the problems, the relationships at home and wider support to the family. Aldridge and Becker (2003) also point out that caring responsibilities may be intermittent. In their study of children caring for parents with mental illness they found that the level of caring tasks varied and were unpredictable because they depended on the state of parents' mental health at that time. The study by Booth and Booth (1998) with 30 now-adult children of parents with learning difficulties found that extra responsibilities were more likely to fall on the child where a parent, usually a lone parent, lacked other support. This is supported by research by Olsen and Clarke (2003) with 60 children of parents with a disability. They found that children of single parents with disabilities were reported as doing more domestic and 'caring' work and that the nature of the activity (in terms of the responsibility it involved even where the amount of work was not heavy) was often different in single-parent families.

Research with children who have additional caring responsibilities shows mixed reactions from children. Jones and others (2002), interviewed 17 young people who had caring responsibilities and found that, for the most part, undertaking additional caring tasks was seen as inseparable from a loving, caring relationship with parents. A study by the University of Stirling (2002), which surveyed 310 children in schools and interviewed six 'young carers' in depth, found that children with caring responsibilities stressed the interdependence of the activities in the household in the context of helping the whole family, including themselves, rather than the notion of helping the cared-for person only. Jones and others (2002) describe an example of a young person who was helping her mother through a serious illness. The young person felt that her part in supporting her mother emotionally and physically during hard times was part of the relationship she had with her mother before she had become ill and that becoming a 'carer' was not something with which she could identify. Aldridge and Becker (2003) suggest that 'young caring' is less about role reversal or attachment disorder and more about role adaptation. Their study suggests that children may take on parenting type roles when parents have mental health problems, but that this may only relate to one aspect of the parent–child relationship.

The study by Jones and others (2002), shows that most families have clear ideas about how children should be parented and that tasks are allocated and balanced as well as possible in order to take account of activities needed for the child's own development. Children are also active players in the process and the study by Olsen and Clarke (2003) provides information about the complex way in which children actively negotiate and resist 'caring' roles. They found that older children are often actively engaged in 'decisions, trade-offs and dilemmas of their own when negotiating caring roles' (p.100). The involvement of younger children (those under ten years old) in domestic and 'caring' tasks was found to be different in this study and parents report having to at times 'fend off' and 'manage' their children's well-meaning attempts to help.

In spite of there being a process of negotiation reported in some families, studies suggest that there are times at which a lack of other support within or outside the family or a crisis can mean that children have little choice in taking on responsibilities. A 12-year-old child quoted in Bilsborrow (1992) from a one parent family said:

> I feel as if I've got to do it and there is no one else to help me.
> *(Bilsborrow, 1992: 24)*

In the study by Liverpool DAAT (2001) all parents and children without exception assumed that older children (13–17 year olds) in a family where there is parental substance misuse would have significant caring tasks and responsibilities.

A study by Strathclyde Centre for Disability Research and Centre for the Child and Society (SCDS and CCS) (1999) undertook a questionnaire with 509 school aged pupils (11–17 years old); focus groups with 12 young people identified as 'young carers' and 12 'young non-carers'; and one-to-one interviews with 14 'young carers'. Interviews with children in the comparison group of non-carers found that children were expected to help with household chores regardless of whether or not there was disability or illness in the family. However, the 'young carers' said they felt a heightened sense of responsibility because the family were relying upon them. One young person said:

> There are times up at the house when you just don't want to be there. You wanna go out but you cannae because things need (to be) done.
> *(SCDR and CCS, 1999: 809)*

Feeling a greater sense of responsibility may not only be associated with providing physical support for ill parents. Children may also feel more responsible if they are trying to support parents emotionally when they are going through conflict or experiencing violence within a relationship (Domestic Violence Advice Line, 1997). In some cases, children may be drawn into mediating between parents (Laybourn and others, 1996). Children who know that parents are going through difficult times can be psychologically protective of them and in the study by Laybourn and others (1996), children reported feeling that they should not talk about their own concerns because this would increase parents' own worries.

> 'Cause she's got all the problems as well, so it wouldn't be fair on her because she suffers from it all.
> *(Laybourn and others, 1996: 164)*

Positive aspects of caring for parents that are reported by children and young people include increased maturity, responsibility, decision-making and practical skills and children may also gain rewards from close and loving relationships with parents (Dearden and Becker, 2000). In the study by Aldridge and Becker (2003), 16 out of 28 'young carers' interviewed in the second round of interviews said their relationship with the parent who was ill was 'good' or 'strong', and ten 'young carers' described improved relationships with the parent. One young person said:

> We are still the best of friends. We do really have a strong relationship and also I feel that I've matured a lot quicker which to me I think is a good thing because I've got a different outlook to a lot of other girls that are my age, you know people are still in school and I think 'My god...'
> *(Aldridge and Becker, 2003: 84)*

In Laybourn and others (1996), most of the children reported disliking their parents' alcohol misuse, however they did report good times with the drinking parent as well as bad. In the long term, one positive aspect of problem drinking was that families could become closer. Other aspects of parental drinking were identified as parents being more affectionate and fun or allowing them more freedom.

Children's education

Children who are experiencing domestic violence in their family, parental substance misuse problems or parental ill health often report that it affects their attendance, concentration or behaviour at school and this may be one of the most visible signs of problems at home (Newton and Becker, 1996). In the case of domestic violence or families that move around, frequently changing school can be a problem. Children can miss out on coursework and exams and lose touch with friends.

Attendance at school can be particularly problematic for children in situations of domestic violence, if going to school will place the family at risk of being found by the abuser. In Mullender and others (2002), one 12-year-old girl said:

> I hate him. We've been in three refuges. When I was in the second one I liked it. One day, when I was coming home from school – he knew what school I was at – I turned round and saw him following me…
>
> *(Mullender and others, 2002: 108)*

Children worry about their parents when they are at school and this is a commonly reported theme across all children's experiences of parental problems. In some cases, children's concentration may be affected to the extent that they report leaving school to check on parents or not attending school regularly because of wanting to remain at home to watch them. Aldridge and Becker (1993) found that most children had missed some school and some had experienced problems at school.

> I skip school because of my mum. I've done it a few times because I'm worried about her.
>
> *(Dearden and Becker, 1996: 15)*

In their later study of parental mental illness, Aldridge and Becker (2003) found that children were particularly concerned that parents' behaviour may result in serious outcomes whilst they were at school.

> I find it worse when I like come home from school and like I'll get a phone call from grandma or someone. Like when I come in. Well most of the time I come in like and nobody will know (mum's) done it (cut her wrists).
>
> *(Aldridge and Becker, 2003: 91)*

Children may also present difficult behaviour whilst at school. Malpique and others (1998), in a study of children whose parents had alcohol problems, found that 11 of the 18 children of school age had difficulties at school and 11 out of 21 reported social difficulties with peers. These problems were associated with aggressive behaviour in the younger children and feelings of rejection and loneliness in the adolescents.

In Dearden and Becker (1996) a large proportion of 'young carers' had educational problems and missed school. The resulting lack of qualifications could exclude young people from the labour market. Providing a large amount of care for parents could restrict children's subsequent career options.

Not all children in these circumstances report having problems at school. In fact for some children the reverse may be true. In order to counteract problems at home they work harder to succeed at school, may find school an escape, some stability in their lives or just a chance to be like everyone else (Frank, 1995).

Making and maintaining friendships

Forming and maintaining friendships can be particularly difficult for children who are experiencing problems at home and this increases their sense of isolation. In the study by Liverpool DAAT (2001), when describing an imaginary scenario one child of a drug-using parent said:

> Other parents warn their kids to keep away from them because
> their parents were smackheads…they would be isolated.
> *(Liverpool DAAT, 2001: 20)*

Children may also fear or experience bullying. This is discussed in more detail in the next chapter. In case studies of children and young people who provided care for relatives, Aldridge and Becker (1993) found that socialising was often curtailed or kept close to home because of responsibilities and this has clear implications for making and maintaining friendships. McGee's (2000) study outlines four main reasons why children that have experienced domestic violence can find it hard to form and maintain friendships. These are that: children are too uncomfortable to bring friends home; the abuser deliberately embarrasses them; they are not allowed to go out; and, finally, that the family moves constantly to get away from the abuser. In addition to the direct effects on children's friendships there were also indirect effects in establishing a social life. Children whose parents have substance misuse problems also report embarrassment about bringing friends home. The study by Liverpool DAAT (2001) highlights that children whose parents have substance misuse problems may also have their play and leisure time disturbed by parents. Importantly this was something children talked in detail about but parents were less aware of and only mentioned occasionally. The importance to children of play opportunities and maintenance of friendships is supported in research with children on the impact of parental alcohol misuse (Laybourn and others, 1996; Brisby and others, 1997).

Summary of key points

- Parents may try to conceal problems at home but children are often more aware of problems than parents realise. This does not necessarily mean, however, that children understand what is happening and why. Some behaviour by parents, particularly associated with domestic violence, substance misuse and mental health problems, can make children feel very frightened and confused.

- The most distressing aspect of parental problems for children is undoubtedly violence and relationship conflict. Children whose parents have experienced domestic violence or have substance misuse problems report witnessing and experiencing a high level of violence and parental conflict. Children report that the impact of conflict is compounded by the unpredictability of parents' moods and behaviour.

- Children, especially older children, actively participate in negotiating roles and responsibilities in their families. However, there are some situations in which children have no choice but to provide physical and emotional support to their parents. Their experiences of providing care and support are complex and individual. Children's roles and responsibilities vary greatly and may be intermittent.

- Children feeling a greater sense of responsibility towards their parents is not only associated with providing physical support for ill parents. Children may also feel more responsible if they are trying to support parents emotionally when they are going through problems.

- Children's accounts reflect that they may experience disruption in their schooling, through missing school, multiple moves or lack of concentration whilst in school. They may also experience problems making or maintaining friends which can further increase their sense of isolation.

3. Understanding children's feelings

Children talk about experiencing a range of feelings when there are difficulties at home. The most commonly reported feelings are love and loyalty, feeling frightened, worried, sad, angry, embarrassed and isolated (Eriksen and Henderson, 1992; Abrahams, 1994; Houston and others, 1997; ChildLine, 1998; McGee, 2000).

Love and loyalty

The strength of children's love and loyalty to their parents comes across in many children's accounts. Children and young people often want to be able to help their parents in any way they can.

> It can get difficult but it's good afterwards knowing I've helped my mum. I enjoy helping my mum, I only wish it could be a bit easier.
> *(Bibby and Becker, 2000: 44)*

Even in situations in which parents are abusive, children's love is often enduring.

> Mum keeps hitting me, she drinks. She won't understand I love her. A girl at school called Mum a slag and a drunk and I hit her and broke her nose.
> *(Houston and others, 1997: 37)*

The following quote encapsulates the dilemma that children may feel when they know a parent's behaviour is wrong but they still love them.

> I can't bear it that he hits her. I feel so ashamed. I always worry that the neighbours will hear or that the teachers will find out at school...I felt really nervous about talking to you, and guilty because my mum and dad are wonderful – they are really good

> people and I don't want you or the researchers to think badly of
> them, because they are very good parents and they love me a lot
> and they have always done everything they can for me. They are
> really interesting people. It's not their fault, it's just the way it is
> with them.
> *(Mullender and others, 2002: 108)*

In an account by Hindle (1998) she describes her work as a child psychotherapist
with one 15-year-old boy. This is only one child's experience and is subjective, but it
graphically illustrates the complexity of the relationships children may experience
with their parents. Kennie's mother had a chronic mental health problem while he
grew up. Hindle describes Kennie's relationship with his mum in the following way.

> Kennie described himself as being close to his mother. He spent
> a lot of time with her, was mindful of her preoccupations, and
> worried about leaving her in case anything happened to her. It
> was clear that Kennie had not only been afraid of his mother but
> had also been inextricably involved with her in what Kennie and
> I came to call 'The Knot'.
> *(Hindle, 1998: 262)*

She goes on to describe the problems that Kennie faced in adolescence as he tried
to gain a perspective on his family and himself and how this was complicated by his
love and loyalty to his mother. In trying to understand his own identity he needed to
move away from his mother, however this was at odds with his mother's need to have
someone with her. Kennie was afraid that if he did not stay with his mother, as she
wanted him to, her illness might return. Feeling restricted in this way and feeling his
mother was not interested in him, he became angry towards his mother.

Fear and anxiety

In the studies on domestic violence and parental substance misuse, children's
accounts show that their fear is first and foremost of violence (towards themselves or
another family member) and parental conflict (arguing and fighting). More than
anything children want to feel safe (Mullender and others, 2002). Experiencing
problems at home can cause children a great deal of worry. This is heightened in
situations in which children fear for their parent's safety because they are
experiencing violence, are at risk of self-harm or if children are concerned about
their parent's ability to care for themselves.

Christensen (1997) reported that daily life for the children in her study whose parents had alcohol problems was emotionally stressful. In research by Liverpool DAAT (2001) children described fear of violence as ever present in homes where there was parental substance misuse. In Hill and others (1996), children in the study reported violence when a parent was drunk.

> *Child:* My mum had a big bruise on her face and big bruise in her leg.
> *Interviewer:* How did you used to feel?
> *Child:* (answers very quickly without visual probes) Horrible, angry and upset.
> **(Hill and others, 1996: 163)**

In cases in which violence occurs, children's fears do not go away even once families have moved away from the abuser, as they may return or threaten to return. Being found again often increases children's sense of powerlessness. The extent of children's fears may show in physical symptoms such as nightmares, sleep deprivation and bedwetting.

> *Interviewer:* What about things like sleep, do you sleep alright now?
> *Young person:* No. I have to sleep watching two doors and with my back against the wall.
> **(Mullender and others, 2002: 111)**

Children of parents with severe mental health problems may also fear that parents may commit suicide if they are left alone.

> I'm frightened to leave her in case she goes into a fit or something. When we were little…she got really down and started taking overdoses and that really scared us…When she's really down she says I'm going to take an overdose…I'm frightened to leave her.
> **(Newton and Becker, 1996: 25)**

Children whose parents experience domestic violence, substance misuse or who are ill report feeling fearful of the future and worrying about their parent's well-being (Frank, 1995; Bibby and Becker, 2000). In the study by Stallard and others (2004) with 24 adults and 26 children, the majority of parents felt that their children had been affected by their illness and half reported their child worrying 'a lot'. Frank's study (1995) interviewed 16 children who helped to support a relative at home. One child said:

> It's not just the caring that affects you…in fact we're a very close
> family and we all pull together. What really gets you is the worry
> of it all, having a parent who is ill and seeing them in such a
> state…of course it's upsetting, you think about it a lot. Someone
> who is close to you and desperately ill is pretty hard to deal with.
> *(Frank, 1995: 42)*

The extent to which children worry about their parents, siblings, themselves and the future of their family comes over very strongly in their accounts. They often seem to carry their parent's worries as their own and prioritise the needs of their parents before thinking about themselves (Ghate and Daniels, 1997). This can be seen particularly in the research on domestic violence and parental substance misuse because family routines and daily life are centred around the mood and behaviour of the adults (Laybourn and others, 1996; McGee, 2000; Mullender and others, 2002). It may also be the case with children and young people who have caring responsibilities. In Shah and Hatton's research (1999) children and young people's accounts demonstrated the centrality of caring in their lives and the extent to which caring responsibilities structured their lives.

 As seen in the previous chapter, children whose parents have substance misuse problems may also feel that their parents are physically or emotionally unavailable when they need them. Studies of helplines show that children often focus on their parent's problems, their needs and their feelings almost to the exclusion of discussing any problems this causes for themselves (Saunders with Epstein, Keep and Debbonaire 1995; Houston and others, 1997). This is supported by the research by Aldridge and Becker (2003) with children caring for a mentally ill parent. They found that 15 of the 40 'young carers' in their study only expressed concerns for their parents' well-being when asked about how their parent's mental illness affected them. One young man said:

> I'm worried in case she goes back to the way she was again. She
> was really bad. She used to cut herself…She don't now. She used
> to either cut herself or take tablets…few years ago now. She's
> been alright for a few years. [It was] horrible.
> *(Aldridge and Becker, 2003: 76)*

Loss

Fear of and experience of loss is another major theme that children discuss. This cuts across all children's experiences of parental problems including children living with parents who have physical or mental health problems. The losses that children experience can be very wide ranging, from losing parents (physically or emotionally) to feeling they have lost their childhood, their homes and possessions or have lost out on opportunities in later life because of the nature of their childhood.

Children are often primarily afraid of losing their parents, either being separated from them through abandonment or social service intervention, through parents separating or through death (Christensen, 1997).

> The psychiatrist said it was an illness that made Mum poorly and
> she would not get better and we would have to be fostered. We
> were frightened and bewildered.
> *(Elliot, 1992: 11)*

Hindle's account (1998) of her work with Kennie describes how he kept secret the details of how his mother had hit him when he was younger for fear he would be taken away from her. Significantly, at the time of revealing this information he was over 16 years old.

Children may feel a sense of loss for parents, usually fathers or male partners, in situations of domestic violence. Ericksen and Henderson (1992) completed a study in Canada with 13 children who had witnessed domestic violence and they report that when children left violent partners in the household they felt relief, pleasure, protectiveness and uncertainty, but some also felt sad because they missed their fathers. In the study by McGee (2000), several children reported finding it difficult to cope with their feelings of loss of their father and in a small minority of cases children may blame the mother for the violence or splitting the family up. The study by Mullender and others (2002) highlights cultural differences in the way in which Asian children in the study viewed their relationships with parents and elders. Children felt that they had to show respect to fathers regardless of their behaviour. One 14-year-old South Asian boy is quoted as saying:

> We go to his shop sometimes, go to the movies. He is okay with
> us, Dad. I have to respect him, not for the violence (but) because
> he is my dad. It is against my religion (not to). I have to respect
> my parents. If I was gora (white), I don't think I would have (to).
> *(Mullender and others, 2002: 148)*

Losing out on childhood because of taking on greater responsibilities within the household and not being allowed time to enjoy being a child, is a theme that frequently appears in literature from children's accounts (Frank, 1995; Domestic Violence Advice Line, 1997) and retrospective accounts from adults.

> I've grown up a lot faster which is good in some ways, but I've
> lost a lot of my childhood. I've missed out on some things.
> **(Domestic Violence Advice Line, 1997: 28)**

> As a teenager I don't think I should do any of it (regular medical
> care) 'cos teenagers are supposed to have fun.
> **(Jones and others, 2002: 19)**

Some children with parents who are ill also report feeling that they miss out on
quality time with parents. A publication edited by Bibby and Becker (2000) is a
collection of children's (aged 8–18) personal accounts of what it is like to provide
care to parents in the home. One 12-year-old girl wrote:

> Dear Mum
> I wish that you and me could spend some more time together
> sometimes...
> **(Bibby and Becker, 2000: 57)**

Children, particularly those whose parents misuse substances also describe missing
out on, or experiencing disruption on special family occasions, such as birthdays and
Christmas (Velleman and Orford, 1999).

Sadness, isolation and depression

Sadness, isolation, depression and in some cases suicidal feelings are expressed by
children across all the literature (Malpique and others, 1998; Dearden and Becker,
2000; McGee, 2000). Research by Strathclyde Centre for Disability Research and
Centre for the Child and Society (1999) used a global depression scale, the
Rosenberg self-esteem scale and questionnaires related to self-concept and quality of
life. Analysis showed that young people who looked after a disabled relative were
more depressed and had lower self-esteem than those young people who did not.
Although it would be hoped that suicidal feelings affected a very small minority,
these feelings are reported in several studies. In a study that talked to 11 children
with caring responsibilities, one 14-year-old girl was quoted as saying:

> I was about 13 or 14 when I took an overdose and everything
> because I didn't want to go home no more. I just hated life...
> I was so young and my freedom was just cut off completely.

> I couldn't go out and nothing like when I came home from
> school...I look after my brother and everything.
> *(Newton and Becker, 1996: 25)*

Similarly, in the study by Shah and Hatton (1999) with 19 children and young
people, a 20-year-old girl said:

> I think I was about 15, I didn't know at the time but I was doing
> everything, and she [mother] was in bed all the time and she
> wouldn't eat and that's when I realised, but I didn't realise, I took
> it out on myself, I thought it was me, I was having problems at
> school and life basically. I felt suicidal, it was that bad, I wasn't
> sad I was totally acute depressed.
> *(Shah and Hatton, 1999: 44)*

In Houston and others (1997), another child whose parent had alcohol problems said:

> I feel sad, like I shouldn't be living.
> *(Houston and others, 1997: 26)*

Feeling lonely is also reported in studies if children feel they have no one to talk to
and share problems with (Bibby and Becker, 2000). In cases of domestic violence
and substance misuse, children may have to deny the behaviour at home in order to
protect parents and this can make them feel confused and trapped. Children who
live with domestic violence or parental substance misuse also fear facing denial or
disbelief if they do tell (Saunders with Epstein, Keep and Debbonaire, 1995).

Anger and frustration

Some children report feeling angry and frustrated at times with their parents or
their situation. One child in the Domestic Violence Advice Line study (1997) says
they felt:

> Angry. I tried to help but always got shouted at...tried to stop
> them arguing.
> *(Domestic Violence Advice Line, 1997: 26)*

Some children in cases of domestic violence may also feel angry at mothers for not
acting to get them away from the violence.

Children may also externalise feelings by acting aggressively towards others (McGee,
2000; Mullender and others, 2002). In the study by Liverpool DAAT (2001), children
said that children in an imaginary family where there was substance misuse would:

...fight more than other kids. The eldest would have to take responsibility and would have to present herself as a figure of authority, the other kids wouldn't respect her and she would get frustrated.

(Liverpool DAAT, 2001: 17)

Guilt, shame and stigma

Several studies have found that children feel guilty about their parent's experiences believing that they themselves have caused the problems (Saunders with Epstein, Keep and Debbonaire, 1995). Christensen (1997) found that children were more likely to feel guilty about parents problem drinking if parents denied the problem. In the study by Laybourn and others (1996), however, guilt was not a recurring theme. Several children reported that parental drinking was due to their behaviour, whereas others thought it was a cyclical process. Children said they thought their parent's problem drinking made children feel depressed and behave badly and then in response their parents drank more alcohol. In studies of domestic violence it seems that younger children were more likely to attribute blame to themselves and to think that this meant that they could stop their parent's behaviour.

Some children who live in families with domestic violence or substance misuse talk about feeling embarrassed or ashamed about the way their parents' behave (McGee, 2000; Mullender and others, 2002). Children whose parents were chronically ill also report not liking feeling 'different' (Frank, 1995). Some responsibilities, particularly undertaking intimate care tasks, can make children feel embarrassed.

> Sometimes I help her to get dressed and undressed to go to bed, if she goes to bed before me...it's slightly embarrassing helping your mum when she hasn't exactly got clothes on.
>
> *(Dearden and Becker, 1996: 22)*

Children whose parents have experienced domestic violence, substance misuse and ill health reported that embarrassment or shame could act as a barrier to talking to other people about experiences. Children in Aldridge and Becker's study (2003) reported being very aware of the stigma associated with mental illness. Twelve of the 40 children reported experiencing stigma in school, amongst friends and in the community. Other children deliberately kept quiet about their parent's illness or reported feeling there was no one they could trust to talk to. Some children also reported being bullied because of it.

> They (local youths) used to bully, they used to bully us. Well they
> used to bully me. And hit, and punch me and everything, when,
> when my dad was watching, and he couldn't really do anything,
> 'cos like they're all faster…and their mum used to come up and
> start shouting at us…Well, like [they would say] 'You look after
> your mum and dad, ha ha', all that. And they would go 'At least I
> haven't got a mental dad' or something.
> *(Aldridge and Becker, 2003: 81)*

In Shah and Hatton (1999), South Asian children and young people with caring
responsibilities talked about experiencing negative reactions to parents with mental
health problems from people in the community. The reasons they thought people
had negative reactions were: cultural attitudes and beliefs about disability and
mental illness; and ignorance and fear.

> I think Asians think it doesn't happen, they think it's a curse,
> witchcraft, they think there's no clinical reason for it. I think that
> the people in my street they act a bit different to my mum, they
> know that she's been in hospital so they think she will do
> something to me, or how is she going to act if I talk to her?
> They're afraid, they don't know what she's really like.
> *(Shah and Hatton, 1999: 54)*

Worryingly, 14 of the 19 children and young people in their study said that they had
been bullied at school. In these cases, bullying seemed more related to racism than
to being a carer; however as the authors point out, children were also reluctant to
discuss caring responsibilities at school and were unlikely to seek support at school.
The reasons children gave were: not wanting to be an object of pity; not wanting to
be seen by friends simply as a 'carer'; fear of being bullied; and fear that children
and teachers may not understand.

Summary of key points

- The accounts that children give of their relationships with parents reflect the
  complexity of their situations. They may have very close relationships with
  parents and their sense of love and loyalty to parents is often very strong and
  enduring, even in some cases where parents are violent or neglectful. Some
  children may feel torn between feeling love and loyalty to parents and feeling
  hurt, angry, embarrassed or resentful.

- Children worry about their parents much more than may be recognised. This is heightened in situations in which children fear for their parents' safety (for example, if parents are experiencing violence or are at risk of self-harm) or if children are concerned about parents' ability to care for themselves.

- Children's accounts demonstrate how the life of the family and the child's own concerns can become centred around the adults who are having the problems in these households, particularly in those families where there is domestic violence, substance misuse or mental health problems.

- The losses that children report experiencing can be very wide ranging, from losing parents (physically or emotionally) to feeling they have lost their childhood, their homes and possessions to feeling they have lost out on opportunities in later life because of the nature of their childhood.

- The sadness and isolation that children may experience can be perpetuated by the stigma and secrecy that surrounds domestic violence, parental substance misuse and parental ill health. In some cases, children may feel depressed or experience bullying.

4. Understanding children's coping strategies

As we have already seen in the previous chapters, children are not passive but active participants in family dynamics and have strong views and feelings about what is happening within their families (Laybourn and others, 1996; McGee, 2000; Mullender and others, 2002). Research findings in this chapter are supported with additional studies that examine children's worries and well-being more generally. The chapter does not cover research with children whose parents have chronic health problems, as their coping strategies are not reported in the literature in the same way. Although children whose parents are chronically ill may not have to cope with the same degree of conflict in the family, they may have to deal with very difficult emotional situations and may have to provide support and help for parents. The literature gives very little information about what coping strategies children use if they provide day-to-day support to a parent.

Use of different coping strategies

Research with children suggests that their coping strategies vary and they may use different strategies to deal with different situations. Children within the same family may not deal and react to problems at home in the same way (Mullender and Morley, 1994; Hester and others, 1998; Mullender and others, 2002). Children's strategies for coping with, for example, domestic violence may be very diverse and often seem contradictory, for example, being very protective and staying at home as much as possible to running away or keeping out of the house (Hester and others, 1998). Although children may use different coping strategies, there are a number of common ways in which children report dealing with problems at home regardless of the type of parental adversity they experience. This may be because the number of options open to children in situations is limited (Velleman and Orford, 1999). A review that looks at the support needs of families who have drug-using members shows that no one style of coping can be seen as the most appropriate and that coping styles may change over time (Bancroft and others, 2002).

The reasons why some children are more or less affected by problems at home are still not fully understood. Studies with children often show that in spite of experiencing trauma in childhood, many children cope remarkably well and overcome difficulties. The study by Mullender and others (2002) reports that in a group interview children said:

> We all cope in all sorts of ways…but lots of children are good at it. Children don't necessarily get upset and in a state about it. They can do fine with it. Some do get upset and they need support and caring because it is such a big thing. It is definitely really a big thing for children.
> *(Mullender and others, 2002: 120)*

Research that has asked children about the coping strategies they use, suggests that the types of coping strategies, for example either inward or outward looking strategies, may vary according to a number of factors. We do not know a great deal about why children in these situations use different strategies and the outcomes for the children. In research that has sought children's accounts about their coping strategies it seems that key determinants of the way children cope include their personality, their gender, their age and their culture. A study by Fuller and others (2000) interviewed 86 young people aged 13 to 14 living in Scotland. Many young people said that the way in which they handled problems would depend on the kind of person they were. There appeared to be distinctive coping styles, identified as the 'independent', the 'isolated' and the 'integrated'. The way young people dealt with their problems was sometimes influenced by the advice or coping strategies of their siblings or friends, who encouraged them to take a particular course of action. In the study by Laybourn and others (1996) of children's experiences of parental drinking, parents indicated that the children who coped best with the situation at home were gregarious and had outside interests.

The study by Fuller and others (2000) highlighted gender as a component in the way children cope with problems. The first sample comprised 22 boys and 33 girls who attended two mainstream schools; the second, 16 boys and 15 girls in residential units. The study found that telling someone about their problems was the most commonly used strategy. They also found a consistent pattern highlighting that girls worry more than boys, that boys are more likely to use avoidance as a coping strategy and less likely to talk about problems. This is supported by other studies that have also found girls to be more able to talk to their friends about problems than boys and to rely on them more for emotional support (Butler and Williamson, 1994; Ghate and Daniels, 1997; Morrow, 1998; Frosh and Phoenix, 1999). Butler and

Williamson (1994) undertook a study of 190 children and young people from local authority children's homes, schools, and youth clubs. They found that, although many boys were adamant they would sort things out on their own, they were often not confidant they could do it constructively. Rather than talk about problems, they were more likely to use other coping strategies to distract themselves. Young boys said they were likely to 'run and hide' to bedrooms or computer games, whilst older boys were more confrontational and emphasised a need to fight back or stand up for themselves.

In the study by Mullender and others (2002) on domestic violence, the strategies children reported using varied according to their age and ethnicity. They found that older children were more likely to have intervened in conflict than younger children and that South Asian children were less likely to have intervened, although on occasion they had done so. Research on substance misuse suggests that younger children are more likely to believe that they can influence their parent's behaviour than older children (Laybourn and others, 1996). Kroll and Taylor (2003) discuss children's use of 'magical thinking', that is the belief younger children may have that they can make or prevent things from happening, and therefore also put them right and regain control. Older children may also be more likely to react by externalising problems, becoming more violent and aggressive in the home or at school or with peers. This aggression may get young people into trouble, in fights or causing physical damage to property. In Fuller and others (2000), young people in residential care used more extreme coping strategies than those who lived at home including truancy, smoking, drinking, taking drugs, smashing things or harming themselves deliberately.

Children's religious beliefs may also help some children to develop resilience and cope with problems. In Mullender and others (2002), a South Asian boy discussed how his religion helped him cope with the domestic violence in his family.

> My religion kept me going. We believe that your time on Earth is full of tests. If you survive, your patience and strength will end your suffering. These are my tests. I had to stand by my mum because she was not in the wrong. That pulled us through and made us stronger and better. We have been through a lot; we can feel for others and are better human beings.
> *(Mullender and others, 2002: 150)*

Coping strategies children say they use

Research on domestic violence and parental substance misuse has found that children describe both psychological (or emotion-focused) and physical (problem-focused) strategies to help them cope (McGee, 2000; Kroll and Taylor, 2003). Some of these strategies are short term whilst others are longer term. In examining the literature across the different types of experiences covered in this review, there were four main types of coping strategy that were commonly reported. These were avoidance/distraction; protection/inaction; confrontation, intervening and self-destruction; and positive action and help seeking (including talking to someone).

Avoidance/distraction

Avoidance and distraction are commonly reported coping strategies. This is significant because children who avoid confronting or talking about problems are even harder to identify, making them less likely to receive any kind of support. Use of this strategy may therefore perpetuate their isolation.

Avoidance was identified by Velleman and Orford (1999) as the most common coping strategy reported by young adults that grew up in families with problem drinkers and children report similar strategies in cases of domestic violence (McGee, 2000; Mullender and others, 2002). Children may physically avoid being in the same environment if there are problems. Mullender and others (2002), reports that children may have a 'haven' to go to. They may either have worked out somewhere they can go if things at home are difficult or escaping the home environment may be an unconscious mechanism. A 'haven' might be the house of a friend, relative or neighbour where the young person knows they can just call in if they want to get away. Often children may just want somewhere they know is safe and supportive. Children may also go somewhere they know they can be on their own or have time to themselves.

> ...because your life can just be tangled up with your parents and you are worrying about them all the time so it's good if you can get away and just be you...
> *(Mullender and others, 2002: 127)*

Children may also psychologically avoid thinking about problems. Many children will deal with the problems at home by trying to ignore them as much as possible, shutting themselves away (emotionally, physically or both) and blocking them out. They report refusing to talk, wanting to be left alone, going out, hiding or staying in the bedroom.

> Yeah, sometimes when I'm feeling a bit down and I think about
> it, it does make me cry, but otherwise it just doesn't because I just
> kind of try to blank it out really.
> *(McGee, 2000: 105)*

These strategies are echoed in the study by Mullender and others (2002) on children's experiences of domestic violence. Children's responses include: 'trying to ignore it, not to hear it', 'pretending you are not there', 'I blank it out, block it', 'hiding from everyone', 'not talking, being withdrawn', 'I put my head under the bed clothes', 'I hide away in cupboards or under beds'. They report that hiding was a frequent strategy used by children and acted as a psychological means of coping and a practical one as they tried to keep themselves safe.

In Fuller and others (2000) young people reported frequently using distraction and avoidance tactics (such as listening to music) and strategies to release their feelings (such as crying). More boys than girls indicated that they would watch television or pretend to others that everything is fine, while more girls than boys indicated that they would cry or write their problems in a diary. In Christensen (1997), a ten-year-old girl said:

> I cry...she says she will quit, but it never quite happens.
> *(Christensen, 1997: 30)*

The following quote is the response of an 11-year-old boy about how he deals with problems.

> Don't talk to anyone – just go off in a mood or watch TV. They
> wouldn't listen. Don't need anyone.
> *(Butler and Williamson, 1994: 70)*

Similar strategies are reported in Mullender and others (2002). Some children in the study reported trying to keep themselves busy during situations of domestic violence by doing some activity, often something that generated noise to block out the sound of the attack. Activities children might undertake are 'watching TV, or playing on the PC or playing music until it's over'. Some children also tried to distract themselves, for example by throwing themselves into schoolwork or other social activities that provide them with a distraction and an opportunity to enhance their self-esteem and confidence.

Younger children also report finding comfort by talking to soft toys, pets or escaping to imaginary places (Ericksen and Henderson, 1992). In the study by McGee (2000), one child said:

> But at least I had one person who cuddled me and that was my
> big dog that I used to love…I'd say something (to my dog) like
> thank goodness that we've got someone who is going to care for
> me and not fight all the time.
> *(McGee, 2000: 106)*

Pretending that everything is well at home and putting on a brave face when there are problems is another way children may cope, particularly if they feel under pressure to maintain a family secret or if they fear intervention in the family. Barnard and Barlow (2003) explain how children go to great lengths to deflect attention away from their own lives, even to the extent of making up stories about birthday and Christmas presents, covering up for parents' behaviour and lying about their home life.

Protection/inaction

Children may protect themselves and their parents/siblings in a variety of different ways. One of the strategies reported regularly is keeping watch on parents. This is discussed in studies of parental alcohol misuse and parental mental illness where children may be worried a parent will drink or harm themselves or others. Similarly, in cases of domestic violence, children may monitor parents' movements in order to know where they are, what they are doing and when. In Aldridge and Becker (2003) a 13-year-old child talks of watching his mother, but it is not clear whether he does this to protect her or himself.

> I usually, like, watch her (mum) a bit more when she's feeling
> depressed. Half the time I don't realise I'm doing it, but I do.
> *(Aldridge and Becker, 2003: 71)*

Children might stay home from school or not go out with friends in order to keep a watchful eye on parents. Laybourn and others (1996) found that this was more likely to be a strategy used by girls. Children may also watch the movements of an abuser if they are aware of the signs that lead up to violence. They may try to behave well so they do not provoke an attack, for example sitting very still or quietly. In cases of domestic violence, children report trying to stay awake at night in case of problems, protecting siblings from being hurt or from hearing what is going on and trying to comfort their mother after an attack (McGee, 2000). In Mullender and others (2002), one girl is reported to 'guard' against the violence of her father.

> Yes that's what I do – I lie awake at night. I still do. I make myself
> be awake so that I can jump up when it's happening and get
> between them. I make myself be awake. Every night I do that.
> Usually it helps because I get between them and cry and try to
> stop them and then my dad does, because he wouldn't want to
> hurt me and gets embarrassed that I am seeing it and that I am
> awake, so I can stop them that way. So it's important that I don't
> go to sleep for my mum's sake…
> *(Mullender and others, 2002: 121)*

Studies also report that children may try to ally themselves with the abuser or think about ways in which their mother could try to protect herself, for example being submissive.

Children may also take protective action such as hiding their money and possessions, in cases of parental substance misuse. They may indulge parents by, for example, giving them money or making them feel comfortable. Children may also use inaction to protect themselves because although they may want to protect other family members they are too afraid of the consequences. This can cause children to feel a tremendous sense of guilt.

> About a fortnight ago he got into bed early with me one
> morning, and he woke me up. All of a sudden he said, 'Mummy I
> am really sorry I didn't stand up for you when Daddy used to hit
> you but I was only little and I was afraid'…
> *(McGee, 2000: 109)*

Confrontation, intervention and self-destruction

Research shows that when there are problems in the home children may try to intervene directly (Abrahams, 1994; McGee, 2000). There are a number of different ways they may do this. In the study by Mullender and others (2002), the way in which most children reported intervening was by shouting; few had tried to physically get between parents. Other ways in which they tried to stop violence occurring were by staying in the room to prevent it, returning aggression, or taking responsibility for arguments.

In situations where children know their parents are desperately unhappy they can feel extremely powerless, frustrated and angry (McGee, 2000). Children's responses to situations where they feel powerless can be intense and frightening, for example having thoughts about killing a parent or themselves. In the study by McGee (2000) on domestic violence, one child reported keeping an air rifle under the bed. The following quotes show some children's responses.

> I hate the bastard. He comes in drunk and hits me and my sister for no reason, he's not the same person. I would like to hire an axe murderer and kill him, but I haven't got enough money.
> *(Houston and others, 1997: 24)*

> I'd like to kill him.
> *(Saunders with Epstein, Keep and Debbonaire, 1995: p.47)*

> Mum tried to keep a quiet life, tried to keep the peace…My brothers are quite big and strong. They were always stepping in to stop it. I was worried one of them would kill him.
> *(Velleman and Orford, 1999: 125)*

In studies with children whose parents have substance misuse problems some children report intervening directly by the dispensing of alcohol and drugs. Children may also use psychological strategies to try to make parents stop misusing substances, for example they may try to ridicule the parent in an attempt to embarrass them or hope that if they show they are unhappy parents will notice and change their behaviour.

Help seeking and action

Research shows that one, if not the most common of coping strategies discussed by children is telling someone (Ericksen and Henderson, 1992; Velleman and Orford, 1999; Fuller and others, 2000) (see next chapter for further discussion). In situations of domestic violence or abuse children may seek help at the time of the attack. They may go to or telephone a neighbour, friend, relative or the police. In Mullender and others (2002), a common strategy was calling the police.

> Try and get the police if it gets really bad. Get a grown-up to phone them if you don't feel able to. But remember the police can be more trouble than they are worth. If you are going to call the police…good to have talked about it with your mum first.
> *(Mullender and others, 2002: 127)*

Children in the same study wanted adults to take the responsibility for the situation, they wanted them to intervene and stop the violence. Children also thought about ways they could act positively to help parents.

> I'm doing everything I can to help her to get more courageous. We could change it around to take out all the terrible memories for her. We've got all our friends there to help. We could get a guard dog. That's what I'd like to do – help her be stronger…I want to make an effort to help her…I want to help out with the washing-up.
> *(Mullender and others, 2002: 117)*

Children said that they thought they would have coped better if they had been engaged in talking about problems. Mullender and others (2002) state that: 'another key element in facing trauma of any kind involves being able to be directly involved in finding solutions' (p.119). They cite Grotberg (1997) who suggests that encouraging children to have supportive interactions with adults, that encourage autonomy, development of personal communication skills and a sense that they are important, will be listened to and taken seriously, enhances children's resilience and ability to cope.

Summary of key points

■ Children may use a combination of coping strategies or may use different strategies at different times or in different situations. Children within the same family may not deal with and react to problems at home in the same way. We do not know a great deal about why children in these situations use different strategies and the outcomes for children. What children say about their coping strategies' suggests that factors such as personality, age, gender, ethnicity and peer group may all be influential.

■ A commonly used coping strategy is avoidance or distraction. This is significant because children who avoid confronting or talking about problems are even harder to identify and so less likely to receive any kind of support. Use of this strategy may therefore perpetuate their isolation.

■ Other common strategies are taking positive action (including talking to someone about problems), protecting family members and intervening in some way.

■ Children say that involving them in discussions and enabling them to play an active role in thinking through and finding solutions helps them to cope better.

5. Understanding children's support needs

Research with children shows that many of the messages they want to pass on about the kind of support they value are the same, irrelevant of the kinds of problems they are experiencing at home. This section looks at messages children give about support in general and then examines informal and formal support more specifically. It draws on broader literature on children's help-seeking behaviour as well as information from specific studies on domestic violence, parental substance misuse and parental ill health. There is very little research, however, that asks children whose parents have health problems who they talk to and what kinds of support they value.

Supporting children

Not wanting to talk to anyone

Not all children receive support, whether informal or formal. Research with children often shows that a significant proportion of them will not feel able to talk about problems whilst they are experiencing them. This is reported in research on domestic violence, parental substance misuse and in wider literature on children's experiences (Butler and Williamson, 1994; Domestic Violence Advice Line, 1997). Butler and Williamson (1994) report that over a quarter of the 190 children and young people in their study said they would not talk to anyone. Similarly, research with children that have been abused shows that many children will not tell (Wattam and Woodward, 1996).

Children give a number of reasons for not talking to anyone. One reason for children in situations of domestic violence or abuse not talking is that they may be afraid of the abuser and how they will react when they realise a child has talked to someone. Clearly, this may be particularly frightening for a child if the abuser has threatened them. The following quote is from a 17 year old in McGee's study.

> So we'd talk occasionally but I was too scared of what to say
> because if it ever got back I knew that I'd be the one that got in
> trouble.
> *(McGee, 2000: 205)*

As well as fearing the abuser, children may also be afraid of the consequences for parents of telling, particularly about violence or illegal activity such as drug misuse. In Barnard and Barlow (2003) a 15 year old is reported as saying the following when talking about her parents' drug misuse.

> *Interviewer:* Did you ever talk about your Mum and Dad to
> anyone?
> *Respondent:* No, it would've got them into trouble wouldn't it.
> There are so many things I had to keep quiet so I just didn't
> bother to say anything in case I let something slip out that I
> shouldn't have done so whenever they started talking about
> things I'd just say I didn't know.

Children may be told by parents not to tell others or they may be scared that the family may be split up and they may be removed from their parent's care. Children may also be worried about how talking about problems at home may affect other people. The following example is from a study on sexual abuse.

> I didn't tell anyone because I was frightened of him. I did not
> want to hurt the rest of the family. There was my grandmother to
> think about and I did not want anyone to know…I knew it would
> cause disruption but fear was my biggest deterrent.
> *(Baginsky, 2001: 77)*

Children may also fear that if they do tell they will not be believed. Some children report a deep distrust of others, including friends and family. The following quote is from a child in Butler and Williamson's study (1994).

> I don't tell nobody 'cos I can't trust anyone in my life any more.
> No one believes me. There's no point.
> *(Butler and Williamson, 1994: 70)*

Other children in this study reported not talking to anyone because they had no confidence that even if they could trust someone else they would be able to help them sort things out. Children may see themselves as the only person capable of changing a situation and therefore take the full burden of worry upon themselves.

> You have to try and sort things out yourself before it gets worse.
> There's no other way.
> *(Butler and Williamson, 1994: 70)*

Children whose parents experience problems often worry about being stigmatised and seen as different. They may be afraid of being teased or bullied if people know about the problems in their family. In the study by Barnard and Barlow (2003) four young boys aged eight to nine years did not mention their parents' drug misuse in the interview even though two of them were reported to know about it. Children who have been abused may also find it very difficult to talk to anyone because of fear of stigma and taboos, particularly those surrounding sexual abuse. Wattam and Woodward (1996) argue that children that tell about abuse, especially sexual abuse, are in the minority and that they are more likely to tell decades later.

As was touched upon in the previous chapter, boys are reported to talk less about their problems than girls. The way in which girls create, maintain and operate friendships is thought to be substantially different to the way boys do (Hey, 1997).
A study by Burman and others (2003) used a questionnaire to 671 girls, focus groups with 89 girls and individual interviews with 12 girls (all 13–16 years old). They described their friendships as the most important thing in their lives. The study reports that girls express their emotions and confide more, are more reciprocal, more mutually supportive, empathetic, nurturing and intimate and more disclosing of information than boys. In Osbourne's study (2001) with young people that had experienced abuse, the boys interviewed who lived in a residential centre did not feel that talking to their peers about intimate issues would be acceptable. MacLeod and Barter (1996) found that boys felt a social pressure to deal with problems themselves and that talking about them may make them look like a 'wimp'. They were afraid that they would be ridiculed or seen as weak if they showed their feelings.

Not talking to anyone about problems at home may also be related to children's ethnicity and culture and fear of racism. Few research studies with children have considered these issues in relation to children's help-seeking behaviour and even fewer have looked at what children with disabilities say about help-seeking. As discussed in Chapter 3, Shah and Hatton's research (1999) reports that 'young carers' in South Asian communities have experienced stigma and racism within their communities and that this can be a barrier to them seeking support. In Mullender and others (2002), the experiences of black and minority ethnic children and children with disabilities were included. They interviewed 14 children who were mainly of South Asian descent and Muslim. They found that children and young people were generally influenced by considerations of family honour (the concept of *izzat* – a patriarchal notion indicating honour, reputation, respectability or status) (Southall Black Sisters, 1993, quoted in Mullender and others, 2002). It was often girls who mentioned this, which fits with it being seen as primarily the responsibility of the woman to uphold the family honour.

> He wanted to keep us under his control – that is why he
> terrorised us. Mum stayed so long because of us and because of
> izzat, you know. 'What will people say?' She hid it from her family
> – wouldn't tell them how bad things were for such a long time.
> *(Mullender and others, 2002: 141)*

Characteristics of people children choose to talk to

Who children talk to about problems depends on the child, on what options they have available to them, what the problem is they wish to discuss and what they want out of talking to someone (do they want to just offload their feelings, do they want to discuss possible options or do they want action taken?) (Butler and Williamson, 1994). Research by Westcott and Davies (1995) was undertaken with a community sample, identified via schools. It was with 98 children (aged 8–17 years old) and focused on the subjects of bullying and parental conflict. It found that children gave a great diversity of responses about why they would choose to talk to someone. It seemed that the most important factors were the helper's ability and willingness to help, their experience of similar situations to those facing the child and their ability to make the child feel better. However, the perceived qualities of the helper were more important than children's own specific needs (Westcott and Davies, 1995). Having an understanding of children's specific experiences may also be a secondary attribute that children appreciate. Research with children whose parents have an alcohol problem suggested that it was important to them that professional helpers understood children's specific experiences (Christensen, 1997). The research by Liverpool DAAT (2001) highlighted that children who attended services with their parents really appreciated kindness by staff and that this made a significant difference to them.

Being listened to is extremely important to children and the research by Westcott and Davies (1995) suggests that children recognise that listening is an active behaviour and they look for signs that demonstrate listeners' attentiveness. The three most mentioned listening behaviours described by children were if people 'look at them', 'try to help' and 'share your feelings'. 'Look at them' was the top behaviour for children aged 8–9 and 10–11 years, whilst 'try to help' was highest for the children in the 12–17 years age group. Butler and Williamson (1994) also report that children in their study said they would trust someone who smiled a lot, had a sense of humour, maintained a lot of eye contact, did not interrupt and appeared engaged and interested in what they were saying.

The study by Butler and Williamson (1994) says that girls reported that they preferred the person providing help or support (whether informal or formal) to be female. Westcott and Davies (1995) also found that female helpers were preferred overall, however girls chose more female helpers and boys more male helpers. In Garley and others (1997), one young man said he found it easier to talk to girls about his mother's depression because they were more understanding. The research by Westcott and Davies (1995) found that younger children were more likely to choose someone to help them from within the family. Research by Mullender and others (2002) suggests that ethnicity may also be important and that South Asian children may be more likely to seek help from within their family.

What children want when they do talk to someone

Children's accounts show that when they do talk to someone it is important that they can trust them, talk to them confidentially and that the person they talk to listens, reassures and believes them. Children do recognise they may need to talk to adults sometimes. When they do this, it often has the main function of helping to 'sort things out' and is required at times when problems are of a serious nature (Butler and Williamson, 1994). However, when children do approach adults for help they often report that they do not get the help that they want. In Fuller and others (2000) more children reported negative experiences of confiding in adults than positive ones, which was a disincentive to confide in them further. Adults were reported as exacerbating problems by over-reacting, causing embarrassment, taking over, moralising and/or trivialising matters. These concerns were also reported in Butler and Williamson (1994). In Osbourne (2001) the key to developing trust and good relationships with young people was found to be spending time with them individually and hearing their fears and concerns. Young people were then more likely to disclose abuse and talk to professionals. Children in Fuller and others (2000) said they were more likely to talk to adults when they gave them advice and suggestions rather than just trying to enforce their own opinions.

Studies suggest that once children have talked to an adult about problems they often do not want to lose control of what subsequently happens and want to remain involved in any future decision-making (Hill, 1999). In Butler and Williamson

(1994) children said they felt that once they had talked to an adult they did not feel they had real choices. Several studies have pointed out that although children want to be kept informed, to be asked for their views and help to think about the appropriate course of action, they do not want to take full responsibility for decision-making. A study with 183 children aged 8–14 that asked about their perspectives on family life found that most children thought that it was important to have a say in decisions affecting them but that they did not necessarily want to make decisions on their own (Morrow, 1998). In Mullender and others (2002) children often reported the use of coping strategies that meant that adults would take the final responsibility. In a group interview with children they said:

> Children may want someone to take responsibility for them,
> instead of them doing it…to take the weight off their shoulders.
> *(Mullender and others, 2002: 127)*

However, as seen in the previous chapter, it is helpful for children to remain involved and informed and to encourage them to help find positive solutions to problems.

Informal support

Informal support for children is often overlooked or undervalued yet children use informal support as their main means of accessing help. Informal support may not only be talking, children may also feel supported in other ways, just by being with someone or being in an environment in which they feel safe (Mullender and others, 2002).

The role of parents

Children who have a good relationship with a parent may talk to them about problems they experience. Studies suggest that children are more likely to talk to their mothers than fathers about problems (MacLeod, 1996; Baginsky, 2001). A research study undertaken with a sample of 11–14-year-old boys about how they construct their masculinity found that many of them saw their mothers as more sensitive. They said they were emotionally closer to their mothers than their fathers who they were more likely to have a jokey, but more distant relationship with (Frosh and Phoenix, 1999). Research with children about domestic violence highlights the importance of the child's relationship with their mother; and several studies on domestic violence have found that children say that mothers may be the only source of support available to them when problems occur (McGee, 2000).

> My mum has helped me the most. No one else really talked
> about it very much apart from my mum. I can't really think of
> anyone else who has helped me apart from my mum. All the help
> was from my mum, she explained everything.
> *(Mullender and others, 2002: 211)*

However, children can also experience problems with trying to talk to parents. As seen in Chapter 2, children may be more aware of what is going on in the home than parents realise and this can mean that parents underestimate the impact on the child. Children may not talk to parents because they do not feel it is their place to, they are rebuffed when they mention it or they are too scared to talk about it. In Barnard and Barlow (2003), parents rarely openly acknowledged drug use and as children became older, parents reported becoming more anxious about their level of knowledge. Interestingly, however, the least likely reported course of action by parents was talking to children about it. Mullender and others (2002) report that in their study there was a divide between those children who had received explanations while they were living in a violent situation and when they left and those that had not received any explanations. Children generally wanted far more opportunities to talk about what was happening at home. Children in the studies on domestic violence, in particular, stressed that they want parents to talk to them more.

> Grown-ups think they should hide it and shouldn't tell us, but we
> want to know. We want to be involved and we want our mums to
> talk with us about what they are going to do – we could help
> make decisions.
> *(Mullender and others, 2002: 129)*

However, parents do not always know how to talk to their children and how much information it is appropriate to give them. Mullender and others (2002) point out that this is hardly surprising given that professionals and researchers who work in the field may also have uncertainties. Whilst parents may wish to relieve children's anxieties by being open with them about problems, they may also be concerned about telling them too much and causing them to worry. A review of research by Hawthorne and others (2003), about divorce and its impact on children raises these concerns and says that 'in practice parents often find it difficult, or feel it inappropriate, to tell their children what is happening or to involve them in decision-making in the belief that they are better protected from adult affairs'. In McGee (2000) the majority of mothers did not initiate discussions with their children about domestic violence whilst it was happening. They usually felt that children were not old enough to understand and they did not want to upset them.

> I don't know if it's right to say nothing to her, whether I should say, discuss things and get her to see it in a more…get her to see it for what it was. Whether she's too young to be doing that with her, I don't know…I'd like to know how it would affect her and to know what I can do. I don't even know how to talk to her about it, because I don't know whether talking to her would be the right or the wrong thing to do…
> *(McGee, 2000: 98)*

Parents may also find it difficult to talk to their children about problems because of their own feelings. Laybourn and others (1996) found that although parents recognised the need to talk to children about events, they often did not feel able to take this on themselves. Hawthorne and others (2003), report that parents' own distress and anger in situations of divorce may make it hard for them to support children.

Children also may feel bound by fears of upsetting parents if they bring up painful and difficult subjects.

> I'd like to know why my mum is ill and I'd like someone who really knows all about it to tell me. I can't talk to mum about it, she gets too upset.
> *(Frank, 1995: 44)*

In cases of domestic violence some children may remain silent until they feel they are given permission in some way to disclose information (Hester and others, 1998).

Research on children's experiences of parental illness show that a lack of communication with children can lead to misunderstandings. Stallard and others (2004) gives the following example from their study with 26 children of parents with mental illness.

Gill suffered from mental illness and had not been able to explain her illnesses to her 11-year-old daughter. During a recent psychiatric hospital admission, Gill took an overdose for which she needed to transfer to a medical ward. Her daughter was told that her mother had been moved and that she could not visit her for a week. As the girl was not told of the overdose, she surmised that her mother no longer wanted to see her.
(Stallard and others, 2004)

The role of friends

Friends (apart possibly from mothers) were found to be children's biggest source of support in studies on domestic violence and more general studies about children's anxieties. They are also the people children will often approach first for support (McGee, 2000). Mullender and others (2002) point out that adults tend to underestimate the importance of relationships between children, either with friends or siblings. In McGee (2000) children referred over and over again to talking to their friends and feeling better.

I had my friends to talk to and that's all I needed to talk to.
(McGee, 2000: 204)

I feel more happier when I talk about it, than keeping it inside.
It helps me because they know a bit what I've been through and
they know what me mum's been through and it helps a lot.
(McGee, 2000: 204)

Friends may not have the same experience or ability to solve problems as adults but they can provide a 'listening ear', empathy or advice (Fuller and others, 2000). Children are more likely to talk to their friends to sound things out before talking to adults, because they know that when they talk to adults the control may be taken out of their hands. Children are often aware they need to be prepared for this and know in their own minds what they want. In McGee's research (2000) the most important thing about deciding to discuss violence was whether they could trust friends. Saunders with Epstein, Keep and Debbonaire (1995) found that children would talk to friends only when they were sure they would respect their confidentiality. Children were also clear about wanting to avoid stigma and not being judged or stereotyped. This finding was echoed in Mullender and others (2002) who found that children ensured they chose the friends they talked to very carefully. If children did confide in someone, particularly if they had the same experience and could therefore really understand, this was very special.

Interestingly, the study by Laybourn and others (1996) on parental alcohol misuse found that few children had talked to friends, as was the case in Osbourne's study (2001) on abuse within the family. This study reports that few young people had attempted to talk to friends or adults, including teachers, largely because of shame, anxiety and embarrassment. Many said they would not talk to people who had not had the same experiences themselves. Children tended to begin to talk to others in their late teens when the desire to share their experiences overrode the inhibiting factors.

The role of others – siblings, extended family and pets

Children may feel they can confide in siblings or extended family. Siblings are likely to be of a similar age and both siblings and extended family will know the people involved and have an understanding of the family dynamics. Saunders with Epstein, Keep and Debbonaire (1995) found that the most common trend was for siblings to discuss the domestic violence amongst themselves. However, there may be reasons why children do not feel they can talk to siblings, usually because of a desire to protect them. In a study with 467 children about their experiences of family life, children who experienced parental separation reported that grandparents had a key role as confidants (Dunn and Deater-Deckard, 2001). In Mullender and others (2002), South Asian children were most likely to discuss problems at home with extended family. They also found that time with extended family or parents' friends (usually the mother's friends) gave children an opportunity to have a break from the home environment and could be very helpful, even in situations where families remained in a violent situation.

Pets are also mentioned as being very important to children. This is mainly in the research on domestic violence but the importance of pets to children who are experiencing problems at home has also been documented in relation to experiences of parental substance misuse (McGee, 2000; Liverpool DAAT, 2001; Mullender and others, 2002) and in research on children's perspectives of family life more generally (Morrow, 1998).

Formal support

Research with children consistently shows that they rarely approach professional services as their first point of contact when they experience problems at home. The exception to this may be accessing confidential helplines. In cases in which children do approach professional services they are likely to have talked to someone else informally first and other adults may act on behalf of children in seeking professional advice and support. The reasons that few children talk to professionals are the same as the reasons children give for not talking to anyone. They lack trust in professionals, are concerned about confidentiality and fear intervention in the family and the associated loss of control over the consequences of telling. Many young people in the Butler and Williamson study (1994) reported having bad experiences when confiding in professionals. This is supported by research with young people that run away. Mullender and others (2002) found that one barrier for Asian children in receiving appropriate support was a lack of knowledge and understanding about domestic violence, racism and cultural norms. Shah and Hatton's research (1999) reported that 'young carers' found that some social service professionals held stereotyped views about the 'culture' of young carers, including assumptions that the young people would wish to continue caring without support. Some young people linked this to ways in which some social workers and doctors of South Asian background perceived family roles and cultural obligations.

In the study by Wade (2002) with young runaways, none of the young people expressed their need for support in terms of help from professionals as they did not trust them to be discrete. Wattam (Wattam and Woodward, 1996) argues that this is why so few children self-report to agencies that are not able to offer confidentiality. Paradoxically, they say it is often the most vulnerable children who are most desperate for reassurance of confidentiality. In some cases children may just want to be told about the parameters of confidentiality and recognise a need for there to be limits on it to ensure the safety of children. Parents in the study by Liverpool DAAT (2001) also stressed the need for clarity around confidentiality and child protection so that remits were clear and services did not encourage secrecy.

Finding professional help

When children do want to find help from professionals they may not know where to go. This issue has been highlighted through research with children who have run away from home (Scottish Executive, 2003). In Fuller and others (2000) helping agencies were much better known to those children that had been in residential care than those who had not. Other than family and friends, almost all of those in the sample of children living at home said they would contact either telephone helplines or school (guidance and other teachers). In addition to these sources of help, most of the residential sample would also turn to social workers; Who Cares? workers; befrienders; children's rights officers; and key workers. The sample of children who lived at home said that their reluctance to contact formal agencies was partly due to a lack of clarity about roles (especially of social workers and counsellors) but also about their negative image. Children felt that there was a stigma attached to approaching services. There were three key problems raised about accessing help. These were:

- locating who may be able to help with a problem (most of the at-home sample were unclear about how to contact social workers and counsellors)
- their accessibility once located (people being too busy or hard to find)
- a preference (particularly by girls) for the helper to be female.

Formal agencies were thought to deal with very specific problems and if young people did not have these problems it deterred them from approaching them with their other problems. If children had a serious or embarrassing problem they said they would probably ring ChildLine.

Talking to professionals

Communication between children and professionals is not always straightforward. Children say that it can be difficult to talk to professionals because they do not have the same vocabulary. Research with children has found that 'child abuse' is not a meaningful term that children would use to describe experiences and, similarly, in work with black families in which children had caring responsibilities, the term 'carer' was not found to be one with which children could identify (Butler and Williamson, 1994; Jones and others, 2002). Studies have also shown that children are confused by the term 'domestic violence' and want to know what acts are encompassed in the definition (physical, emotional, sexual acts, arguing, shouting?) and who might be involved in it (men, women, children?) (Burman and others, 2003). Hill (1999), in a research review, highlighted that children would talk more easily to professionals whose roles and styles of communication they are familiar with, for example teachers.

Children also may fear that professionals will make the situation at home worse. This was highlighted in Mullender and others (2002). Asian children feared, and in some cases experienced, professionals making things worse because of a lack of understanding of issues of family honour and their culture.

Children, particularly those whose parents are ill or experiencing domestic violence, report that they can feel ignored by professionals and frustrated at not being involved in decision-making that affects the family. Children who provide care or support for parents often feel that they know a lot about a parent's illness – but they may often not be asked for their opinion by professionals, may not feel listened to, feel ignored by professionals and not involved in decisions that affect their parents and themselves.

> It felt like a constant battle. Right up until recently, the past two years is really when they'll actually start taking you seriously you know and listening to actually what I say and think that perhaps 'well maybe she does know what she's talking about'. But for years, I mean I was told by consultants and people you know 'you're only a little girl, what do you know?' Sort of at the age of 15 I was told this you know it is so frustrating when you're trying to say 'I live with my mother, I see it'.
> *(Aldridge and Becker, 2003: 73)*

Aldridge and Becker (2003) also point out that only five of the 40 'young carers' they interviewed had been included in discussions with statutory professionals.

The process of disclosing information

Disclosing information about problems at home to unknown professionals can be very difficult for children. Children in the study by Mullender and others (2002) stressed the importance of consistency and continuity in support and moving at the pace of the child. In an evaluation of a Family Alcohol Service (FAS) in London, a central issue for children was found to be feeling safe enough to disclose difficult thoughts and feelings. The ability to do this was dependent on the characteristics of the workers and their ability to be sensitive to when and how children wanted to talk. A 16-year-old boy talked about how having the option not to talk about painful things would help you to develop a bond with a worker.

> It's important that [children] feel that they are there of their own will…that if they want a break or somebody makes them upset they don't have to stay. Because if they're there and a subject really hurts them and they feel trapped…the next time they won't go back…in case they feel like trapped in that situation.
> *(Templeton and others, 2003: 37)*

Provision of written information

As seen already, studies of children's experiences of parental ill health show that more age-appropriate information needs to be available for children. The study by Stallard and others (2004) suggests that not all children want to know more and parents do not necessarily want children to have access to certain information. However, for some children who feel anxious about their parent's illness, appropriate information may help to overcome possible misconceptions and help children to communicate more openly with parents. Children in the study by Stallard and others (2004) wanted to understand how their parent became ill (for example, Was it because I was naughty?), their symptoms (for example, Why Mummy sits and stares) and their treatment (for example, What happened to Mummy in hospital?). Segal and Simms (1993) explain that information gives children a sense of control and time to prepare for an unwanted event if parents are ill. Children's imagination may run riot if they are not given accurate information, they may feel left out and may cut themselves off further. Giving children information allows them to make informed decisions about the present and the future. The following quote is from a personal account.

> People tend to protect children and young people. For me this translated into ignoring my need to be informed and involved. My life was affected anyway and if I had guidance it might have made the experience more positive. I needed good, age-specific information about my mother's condition and its consequences. And I needed someone to talk to who would listen in confidence and help me to express and explore the complex feelings and situations I was dealing with.
> *(Marlowe, 1996: 101)*

The report by Shah and Hatton (1999) also highlights this point. Children and young people who were providing care reported that services had a contradictory view of 'young carers'. Service providers did not provide them with information or consult with them about the needs of the person they cared for, yet they expected them to be responsible for the care of the parent.

Studies of domestic violence also highlight a lack of information for children and young people. In McGee's study (2000) children felt that they were not given enough information, particularly about the process when they were involved in a child abuse investigation.

> I don't think I had any security, any knowledge of what was going
> on. I needed to be told everything. I didn't realise that there was
> a chance that I might have been taken away. But I think I should
> have been told a bit later (after the investigative interview) by
> somebody what was going to happen with my dad. But my mum
> was the only person really who told me that.
> *(McGee, 2000: 124)*

Experience of contact with professionals

Children who are experiencing problems at home may come into contact with
statutory and voluntary agencies. There is not a great deal of information from
children's accounts of parental substance misuse and parental ill health about
contact with specific formal agencies. Most of the information we have comes from
studies of domestic violence or more general research on children's experiences.
What does exist shows that reports of children's experiences with statutory agencies
– particularly social services, police and schools – tend to be mixed, with accounts of
contact with social services and police often being fairly negative. Information about
children's contact with voluntary agencies tends to come from research that covers
domestic violence refuges and services for 'young carers'.

Social workers

Some children report positive experiences of intervention by social services. In
McGee (2000), children who were given information and felt their views were taken
seriously were positive. They were appreciative of an approach which concentrated
on building a relationship and that went at the child's pace. The study describes one
case where there was domestic violence and the child had been sexually abused by
her father. The child talked about how the social worker built up a relationship with
her and this gained her trust.

> I think with the social worker and them, like they talk about stuff,
> other things at first so I grow to trust them and then we would
> start talking about stuff like that (the sexual abuse).
> *(McGee, 2000: 126)*

In McGee's study (2000), children's biggest criticism was the lack of information
social workers gave them about what was going on. McGee also notes that although
the children may have been the primary reason for social work involvement with the

family, children's own contact with social workers appeared to be minimal even where there was an allocated social worker. She describes one case in which a mother had concerns about her five-year-old son, but on visiting the family the social worker did not talk directly to the child. Subsequently, it was found that the child had been sexually abused by his violent father. The mother felt that had the social worker talked directly to him he may have disclosed the abuse.

A child in Aldridge and Becker's study (2003) reported that although they had been involved in discussions with a social worker they did not feel their views had been listened to.

> Social services are horrible because they like, they change,
> they're making all these decisions about your life and then they
> keep you in the dark and not telling you about it…No they did
> not listen to any of us…They said like if any of you have any
> questions you want to ask us out of the whole thing just say it. I
> did though it was [sister's] turn and they just told me to shut up.
> *(Aldridge and Becker, 2003: 117)*

Research on the Domestic Violence helpline found that children did not want to talk to teachers or social workers. Young people in Butler and Williamson (1994) said that social worker contact could be irregular, unpredictable and 'never there when you need it'. Many of the children felt that social workers may break promises and confidences and 'spread things around'. They feared that professionals will 'blab', or share information that children do not want others to know. Laybourn and others (1996) found that children who had experienced intervention from social services (usually placement in foster care) did not view this as helpful or a long-term solution to their families' problems. They wanted their parents' alcohol misuse problems sorted out and wanted to be living with them.

Police

Children's accounts of contact with the police in cases of domestic violence or abuse do not tend to be very positive. Children in the study by Osbourne (2001) reported mainly negative reactions to police intervention in situations of suspected abuse. Mullender and others (2002) also report that no child who had come into contact with the police about domestic violence had purely positive things to say. Children said that action taken had been ineffective or that they felt invisible to police even when they themselves had made the call.

> *Interviewer:* When the police came did they ever talk to any of you
> (the children)?
> *Young Person:* No.
> *Interviewer:* And had it been you who had called them?
> *Young Person:* Yeh!
> **(Mullender and others, 2002: 105)**

Children also reported a lack of sensitivity of police and courts to children's needs (Mullender and others, 2002). In McGee's study, teenagers in particular, tended to be critical of the police response to domestic violence. One 15 year old described their response as 'useless', whilst another said calling the police actively made matters worse.

> Usually I wouldn't phone the police because I know that it makes
> it worse. The police just come to the door and then they go and
> leave him in the house, which means that my mum's getting into
> more trouble, I'm going to get in trouble.
> **(McGee, 2000: 141)**

Schools

Research on domestic violence and parental ill health suggests very mixed responses from schools about supporting children who are experiencing difficulties at home. McGee's study (2000) found that 35 of the 54 families had contact with schools and nurseries about domestic violence and 24 of these felt they had a positive response. Few mothers said they felt unsupported by the school, they felt the school should know about what was happening but they did not expect any particular support concerning the domestic violence. Mothers were particularly appreciative when the school referred them on to another agency for support for themselves or their children. However, in 15 cases children spoke to teachers about domestic violence but in only five of these did they say they felt supported by the teacher. Children frequently wanted more practical support from teachers and referrals over child protection concerns were not necessarily followed up. Young people and mothers reported feeling frustrated when children told teachers about domestic violence and they did not do anything.

> I used to tell teachers and my friends at school what he was like
> and they, I could see they believed me but they couldn't do
> anything about it.
> **(McGee, 2000: 145)**

Mothers in the study by Mullender and others (2002) reported a lack of awareness by schools of domestic violence and its potential impact on children, and said that schools had little sympathy for children who experienced learning difficulties and behavioural problems.

Children in the studies of 'young carers' report that schools can be insensitive to the additional responsibility they have at home. Children in the study by the University of Stirling (2002) report that they felt their confidences to teachers were often considered 'stories' or 'excuses'. They thought teachers should be more aware of how their caring relationships may affect attendance at school and the meeting of deadlines.

> I don't think they offer enough support. You have extra to do at
> home so it's possibly harder to meet deadlines and things like
> that but they never recognise that it's always you must get your
> homework in this day.
> *(University of Stirling, 2002: 3)*

A lack of confidentiality and privacy in teacher's practice was seen as a cause for concern.

Domestic violence refuges

Children who have experienced domestic violence tend to speak highly of support in domestic violence refuges. Osbourne (2001) found that children were much more positive about a social worker who worked in a refuge because she spent time with them and listened. This is echoed in both McGee (2000) and Mullender and others (2002). McGee reports that children said over and over again that they had only had the opportunity to talk about what happened to them when they went to a refuge.

> It was good because then you knew what they were going
> through and they knew what you were going through. And you
> could talk about it; there was some girls and another boy my age
> and we used to sit down and talk about it…
> *(McGee, 2000: 166)*

The study by Mullender and others (2002) supports this. Children reported that children's workers in particular paid attention to their needs and that they could tell their story at their own pace and voice their fears. Having this opportunity meant that children could talk their feelings through and gradually make sense of their experiences.

> The child care worker – she was great. If I was upset, she'd ask
> why and make it okay. She'd talk about it with me. The child
> worker was the best.
>
> *(Mullender and others, 2002: 214)*

Children said what they wanted from refuge provision was children's workers who arranged activities, 'took you out of yourself', facilitated discussions about domestic violence, provided support for their mothers and had enough staff so there was always someone available. Asian children and parents in the study who had come into contact with specialist refuges for minority ethnic families were also very positive about their experiences. In McGee's study (2000), children's only criticisms of refuge life were that there should be more facilities for children (not all had contact with a child's worker) and children did not always find communal living easy.

Services for 'young carers'

Research that has looked at 'young carers' projects suggests that they provide an important function and serve to meet children's needs. They are particularly useful in terms of helping children access professional interventions, making decisions about caring and have an important social function for children, allowing them to meet other children in a similar position and gain support from project workers (Aldridge and Becker, 2003). The project workers are instrumental in helping raise children's confidence and self-esteem.

> ...gives me something to look forward to...I did a creative poetry
> workshop...it gets me emotions out, it gets me feelings out and it
> tends to help a lot. It's kind of therapeutic.
>
> *(Aldridge and Becker, 2003: 118)*

Importantly, however, in the study by Aldridge and Becker (2003) project workers could not necessarily offer children specific support in relation to their parent's mental health condition. This was often because they were generic workers and had little or no training in the possible spectrum of health-related issues parents' might experience. Children therefore need to be able to access specialist information from elsewhere.

What services do children say they want?

Very little research on domestic violence, parental substance misuse and parental mental health problems seems to have asked children directly about the types of formal support they would value, so little is known about their perspectives on the most appropriate forms of provision to meet their needs. Currently there are very few specialist services that exist, given the number of children we know are affected by these problems.

As discussed earlier, research suggests that children do not always know where to go for help (Fuller and others, 2000). A report by the Scottish Executive (2003) on young runaways suggests that advertising services in areas where young people congregate should be considered, for example in bus and railway stations. This report recommended that helplines should be promoted as children and young people often favour contacting these initially to obtain advice whilst maintaining control and remaining anonymous.

> I phoned ChildLine twice, just to talk to them really. It's just nice to have someone you don't know who [you] can put all your bits and bobs on to and even, if they don't take it in, as long as they are listening. It's easier to talk to a stranger sometimes because you can let all your real feelings out. You don't have to worry about what they may think of you. You don't have to be afraid of saying something.
> *(Mullender and others, 2002: 217)*

Helplines also often operate outside office hours when children may need support, particularly in crisis situations. However, the report by the Scottish Executive (2003) points out that they need to be provided within a broader programme of support as children report not always being able to get through. Helplines should be able to provide advice but are not a means of long-term support for children so it is important that they are able to put children in contact with local services they can access that have the skills and capacity to provide relevant support.

Research by Laybourn and others (1996) on support for children of parents with alcohol problems found that suggestions for services from parents, children and professionals fell into two main groups. The first group comprises universal services, that is services where children could obtain help without the nature of the problem being visible. Given the stigma that surrounds many of the problems discussed, this is an important aspect of help for children. Examples of services that were given in their discussions with young people, parents and professionals were:

- drop-in centres
- fun activity groups
- a general family service
- an anonymous helpline

- educational initiatives
- befriending.

The second group of services suggested were more specialist. These were:

- individual counselling
- group work
- family mediation
- an out-of-hours crises service.

In Mullender and others (2002), there was a need identified for specialist youth provision for those that have experienced domestic violence; this may be provided via refuges or elsewhere. Parents also said they would like there to be more space for children to do homework (particularly in refuges) and affordable or free after-school programmes. The independence of services from statutory authorities was also seen as important so that parents and children did not feel threatened.

One of the main wishes of children in Laybourn and others (1996) was to meet other children who had the same experience as them. Parents and children also felt that staff of such services should include 'survivors' of parental alcohol abuse. This was supported by research by Christensen (1997) with children and young people whose parents had drinking problems. They said they felt it was important that support for them should be at the same centre that parents attended so that staff understood their situation, knew their parents and were able to provide reassurance. It was also felt to be important that workers had personal experience of the types of problems that children wanted to talk about.

Children's main plea in terms of provision, however, is the need for better age-appropriate information to be available to explain what is going on in their family. This information may come in either verbal or written form but ideally in both. Children also mention in the research the value of having opportunities to enjoy themselves, have a break from problems at home and have time to have fun and gain confidence. They also value opportunities to meet other children in similar situations (Liverpool DAAT, 2001; Mullender and others, 2002; Aldridge and Becker, 2003).

Summary of key points

- Some children will not talk to anyone about their problems. Boys, in particular, find it hard to talk about problems at home. Reasons that children give for not talking about things at home are fear of violence, fear of the consequences of telling (for example, being separated from parents, hurting other people), fear of not being believed, distrust, not feeling anyone can help, and shame and stigma.

- The personal qualities of a helper may be most important to children when choosing who to talk to. Children want to talk to someone who they trust, who will listen to them and provide reassurance and confidentiality. Having an understanding of the specific problems the child is experiencing is also likely to be valuable.

- Children use informal support as their main means of accessing help, however it is often overlooked or undervalued. Children are likely to talk to parents (more often mothers) or friends, siblings or extended family or pets.

- Children rarely seek the help of professionals initially. There are differences in language between professionals and children, professionals may fail to listen or understand children and children may be more likely to disclose information if they feel safe and have built up a relationship with a helper. Experience of contact with professionals is mixed, with key concerns those of being believed, professionals not talking directly to children and not acting to help them when asked.

- Children's most persistent plea is for more age-appropriate information from informal or formal helpers, both verbal and written.

- Children mention a need for confidential support such as helplines, universal and specialist support. Children particularly want opportunities to get away from the home and have fun and to get to know other children experiencing the same problems.

6. Conclusions and implications

We know that many children will experience or witness violence in their home, parental substance misuse and parental health problems. On reviewing the literature it is clear that although children's experiences are all very different, there are many common themes that arise when they talk about their experiences, feelings, coping strategies and what would help make things better.

Only a small proportion of children whose parents experience domestic violence, parental substance misuse and parental health problems will ever come into contact with services. The accounts that are given by children included in this review are largely those of children who have had contact with services. Optimistically we could hope that this is why they reflect in some cases such traumatic and chaotic lives. However, from what these children tell us and from what adults tell us about their childhood, we know that there are many children who will experience these problems but who will remain invisible to both informal and formal sources of help.

The experiences that children describe in the review are mixed. However, children show remarkable strength and resilience and many have strong relationships with one or both parents. The review suggests that policy, service development and research needs to think more broadly than just meeting the needs of children who are known to agencies and should seek to include and understand the voices of children who are living with parents in the community.

Children's preoccupations

At the beginning of the report it was suggested that children's preoccupations might be different to those of adults. The themes that have arisen come from what children have told researchers. It is of course difficult to know to what extent these reflect children's agendas or those of researchers. However, there are key themes that children talk about that are not necessarily fully recognised by adults.

Children do not talk about 'domestic violence', 'parental substance misuse', 'parental ill health' or 'abuse'. Indeed these are not necessarily terms that they understand or can identify with. Similarly, they do not think of themselves as being 'a young carer' or 'a child of a parent with substance misuse problems'. They think about themselves as individuals with different roles and responsibilities within and outside their family. Their accounts reflect the complexity of family situations and their own subjective experiences.

Children report worrying about parents much more than may be recognised by adults. First and foremost children want their parents to be well and happy and they want their family to be safe and free from violence, fear and unpredictability. They want their parents to give them love, security, reassurance and attention. Their accounts show that they are more aware of what is happening in their family than parents think, however this does not mean they necessarily understand what is going on. Children's accounts demonstrate how the life of the family and the child's own concerns can become centred around the adults who are having the problems in these households, particularly in those families where there is domestic violence, substance misuse or mental health problems. In these families, the well-being and behaviour of parents may dominate the organisation of routines and daily family life. Children can become drawn into maintaining secrets and covering up problems at home in order to protect parents and themselves. They may also have to protect parents and siblings from violence, provide emotional support to parents and feel they need to keep quiet about their own feelings and problems because of a need to be strong for their parents' sake.

Children's reactions to problems at home and subsequent preoccupation often seems to be with thinking about and trying to make sense of what is happening in their family and why, and trying to find solutions to problems. Children look for explanations but trying to understand parents' behaviour can be difficult for children and, particularly in situations of violence or self-harm, children can feel frightened and confused. Relationships and dynamics within families are often complex and the way that children feel and react to problems at home often reflects these ambiguities. The accounts children give show that many children have very close relationships with parents and their love and loyalty to parents is often strong and enduring. Many children express a desire to help their parents overcome problems. Some children whose parents are experiencing difficulties, however, may feel torn between love for parents and a dislike of parents' behaviour or the restrictions their problems may place on the children's own social lives and education. The sadness and isolation that children may experience can be perpetuated by the stigma that surrounds domestic violence, parental substance misuse and parental ill health. In some cases children may feel depressed, have problems making or maintaining friends, have disrupted education or experience bullying.

In the case of domestic violence, children's accounts of when they have moved away from abusers show that they have a remarkable resilience and ability to heal from previous bad experiences. Children do not generally spend much time thinking about the past, their preoccupation is usually with making the present and the future better. As seen in Chapter 4, children have a range of coping strategies that they can employ and being involved in problem-solving and subsequent decision-making helps them to feel empowered and active in the process of making their lives better.

Balancing children's needs and responsibilities

The worry that children feel for parents and the role they play in supporting parents physically and emotionally gives rise to the dilemma about how much responsibility children should have. Children's accounts of living in a family with a parent with a physical or mental health problem are mixed. Some children talk about difficult aspects of providing care and support to parents and feel as if they are missing out on social and educational opportunities. However, many children view their help as contributing to reciprocal relationships within the family. This may be more likely to be the case in families in which children's contribution has been negotiated.

Children whose parents have mental or physical health problems or who are going through difficult times may not necessarily undertake more practical tasks in the home than other children, but they may feel more responsible. It is not necessarily about the actual doing of practical tasks (although some children may resent the restrictions this places on their lives) but about being relied on and being the only person there for a parent to talk to. Children's accounts show that this applies as much to children living in situations of parental violence, conflict or separation as ill health. Their experiences cannot necessarily be quantified in terms of the amount or extent of tasks they undertake on a regular basis as it is more about the level of responsibility they feel for their parents and how that responsibility effects each individual. Banks and others (2001) say the shift to a more qualitative approach that considers the subjective impact on children is already beginning to happen. Parents and children need to be given the opportunity to discuss and make choices. Balancing what is appropriate for any child within a family is likely to vary, depending on the family situation and the wishes and abilities of members in the household. The research reviewed throughout the report shows that children are social players in all situations and their roles and responsibilities are often negotiated within families. The situations in which children seem more vulnerable are those where roles are not negotiated and situations occur in which children have no choices. In crisis situations or where parents lack other support mechanisms children may be expected to do more. These are the families that need more targeted support. In providing a package of support, children need to be involved in decision-making as the research shows they may not want to relinquish helping tasks in the family. The study by Olsen and Clarke (2003) supports a need for a more sophisticated approach to the understanding of the place of 'caring' within relationships, rather than it just being seen as a product of parental impairment or absence of formal support.

As was discussed in Chapter 1, the debate about the usefulness of the term and concept of 'young caring' has been had elsewhere (see Olsen and Parker, 1997; Newman, 2002; Aldridge and Becker; 2003; Olsen and Clarke, 2003). The concept has undoubtedly met with huge success in attracting policy and much needed services for children who are often vulnerable and in need of support. However, it should be recognised that these children are not necessarily a discrete group with similar problems and needs (Banks and others, 2001). Care should be taken not to exclude children who may be living in other difficult circumstances in the home, who may provide support for parents in less quantifiable ways. It is also important that the experiences of children whose parents have health problems, but who do not provide additional support to parents are not forgotten. They may have the same kinds of emotional needs and experience the same confusion about their parent's ill health as other children who do provide care.

Children's need for support

At the beginning of the report we highlighted that the needs of children whose parents have problems, such as domestic violence, substance misuse and ill health may be overlooked because the services that these families are most likely to come into contact with are adult-focused. Research suggests that social workers who work with adults, whether in the field of substance misuse, mental health or physical disability may not fully consider or recognise the impact of parent's problems on children (Kroll and Taylor, 2003). However, this is a key point of contact at which these children could be targeted for support.

As the review shows, parents and children are very aware of the stigma that surrounds these parental problems and children may not feel able or want to talk openly about problems in the home. In situations of domestic violence or abuse children may be silenced through fear of the abuser. Children may also fear the response from other children and adults if they confide in them and, perhaps most importantly, they may fear discriminatory responses from service providers. This has been identified as a common problem in families where a parent is physically or mentally ill, as well as in those in which there is domestic violence or parental substance misuse (Aldridge and Becker, 2003). Parents and children feel afraid to ask for help and to be honest about their level of need in case they are not deemed to be able to cope with parenting. Children's invisibility is often also perpetuated by their coping mechanisms. One of the most commonly reported strategies used by children in difficult circumstances is avoiding the problem or distracting themselves.

Making children's lives better

Enabling children to understand problems at home

Lack of communication is a major barrier to children and young people getting the help they need. There are problems of communication within families, between parents and children and between siblings. One cause of this seems to be the shared desire to protect one another. However, despite parents' efforts to protect children, it is clear from the research that children often know more than parents think about what is happening at home. Trying to 'protect' children in this way may therefore be futile. Children and parents need to be encouraged to talk more openly when there are problems at home. This may help prevent misunderstandings and help children to understand why things are happening.

Parents face a dilemma in some of these circumstances about how much information they should provide to children. Parents may appreciate information or professional guidance that helps them to understand their child's stage of development and what level of information is appropriate if they are uncertain.

The research suggests that children often do not or cannot talk to parents and they may prefer to talk to someone else with whom they have a relationship of trust. Children say that they want to talk to someone who will listen and once they have spoken, particularly to friends, they report feeling relieved. In situations in which parents do not feel able to talk to children or they think children may prefer to talk to someone else it may be helpful to ask a member of the extended family or a friend of the family to talk to children. Schools should also be encouraged to develop peer support or befriending schemes for children.

Children lack written forms of communication about problems in the home and the message from many of the studies is that they are desperate to have information in a format they can understand that helps to explain what is happening. Forms of information that encourage parents and children to talk together about problems may help to encourage conversation amongst the family more generally.

Children and parents also need to be better informed about the services they can expect to receive, the thresholds for intervention by social services in families and the standard procedures and processes (in order to try to dispel ungrounded fears about child protection) and what families can do if they do not receive the services to which they are entitled. Providing information to children and parents about the levels of confidentiality that services can offer is also important.

Enabling children to talk about problems at home and to access help

First and foremost children use informal sources of support. They are most likely to turn to parents (usually mothers) and friends, then siblings, grandparents or pets. This support may come in the form of talking or just spending time with someone and feeling safe and secure.

We know that children rarely talk to professionals but may be encouraged to do so, either through helplines or by providing spaces in which children can feel safe. Having time to build up relationships of trust with peers or adults is likely to help them to discuss problems at home. This supports the need for initiatives such as Connexions and for youth work. Teachers are also in a good position to help children to talk about problems.

Children still do not know where to go to get formal help. Seeking to reduce stigma about children's experiences by more informal group discussions in schools and other youth settings may help to encourage children to confide in someone. A digest of local services for children distributed universally via schools or Connexions services might be a way of children being better informed about local service provision.

Listening to children when they do choose to talk about problems is very important because children who do not get a positive response from adults they speak to, may not try to talk about problems again. Professionals that come into contact with children should be proactive in talking to children, particularly if there are signs that they may be experiencing problems at home, for example being withdrawn or unusually quiet. Children's accounts of coming into contact with professionals in relation to domestic violence suggested that, in some cases, professionals did not speak directly to children.

Professionals that do have contact with children should all be aware of how to communicate effectively with them, using verbal cues to show attention and interest and providing children with reassurance. Professionals need to remember not to use jargon when talking to children as they may feel marginalised and disempowered if they do not understand what is being said. These qualities in helpers may be more important to children than those of having a first-hand knowledge of the problems they are experiencing. Talking to people who do have experience of their situation, however, may also be helpful.

The review shows that boys in particular may find it hard to talk about problems at home. They are less likely to talk to someone until nearer crisis point than girls. The problems boys have in accessing services need to be addressed urgently. We do not really understand what would make boys more likely to talk about problems and seek support. More work needs to be done on understanding the types of services boys would approach and developing services in a way that meets their needs. Ensuring that children have a choice of a male or female helper and a helper of the same ethnicity as them may be advantageous.

Respecting children, recognising and valuing their experience and acting on any concerns appropriately

Children's accounts of receiving professional help are not very positive. Children often fear that if they do tell about problems at home, they may not be believed and positive action may not be taken. Children often do not feel confident that professionals will make things any better for them and in many circumstances they are worried that intervention may make things worse.

For social workers working with children there are tensions between listening to the child and considering their wishes, assessing and managing risk and acting in the best interests of the child. If action has to be taken by an adult, this needs to be explained in a way the child can understand and, if possible, they should be involved in any subsequent decision-making. It is also important that professionals working with parents where there are problems ask children for their input. In the case of parental ill health, many children feel frustrated at not being involved in decision-making about the care and support of parents.

Although children do want to be involved in decision-making and want their wishes to be listened to and taken seriously, they may not want to be responsible for making the decisions. In situations in which children have asked for help from professionals it is very important that they show the children they are listening to them; and that action is always discussed in partnership with the children and their families. Helping children and families to find their own solutions to problems is likely to make them feel more in control of situations and may encourage them to participate more actively in making solutions work.

Providing an appropriate range of support

We know very little directly from children whose parents have experienced domestic violence, substance misuse or health problems about the types of formal services they would value. However, it seems that a range of universal and specialist services needs to be available to children and families to meet the diversity of needs. Although there are overlaps in the types of feelings and coping strategies children may use, there are many differences in individual experiences and there is a need for some specialist services that can work with children alongside meeting the needs of their parents. There is an identified gap in services that meet the needs of older children experiencing domestic violence at home and there are very few services designed to meet the needs of children living with parents who misuse substances.

Children's accounts show that their most urgent request is for age-appropriate information about the problems their parents are experiencing. They also talk about welcoming an opportunity to have a break away from home, have some fun and get to know other children experiencing the same problems.

Suggestions for future research on children's experiences

The research that has been undertaken with children on their experiences of domestic violence, parental ill health and substance misuse is largely based on small-scale personal accounts because of the problems accessing children and gaining parental consent. More, larger-scale studies would be useful, as would studies that access children via methods other than contact with services. Most research that has been undertaken with children has only interviewed children at one point in time. This may not accurately reflect children's experiences and feelings and future work would benefit from a longer-term approach that allowed for building a relationship of trust with the child and could monitor the impact on the child over time.

Accounts from children and young people about living with parental drug misuse are a notably absent feature of existing research, as are accounts from children who have parents with health problems but who do not provide support. There is also very little about children's experiences of contact with professionals when there are problems at home and children remain within the household. More research needs to look at the types of support children in these families want, particularly focusing on boys' needs and those of minority groups, including children with disabilities. It is also important that we develop an understanding of the kinds of support that are effective.

There is an absence of research that examines the interface between these problems within the home and other issues such as poverty and social exclusion and how each of these impact upon children. The reasons for children experiencing problems at home when living in families with chronic problems, such as ill health and substance misuse, need to be teased out. The role of other factors on children's experiences remains unclear. Research might also focus on children's coping strategies in terms of ascertaining whether there is any link between the types of coping strategies used and short- and long-term outcomes for children.

For a summary of research that is under way in these areas, in the UK, see Appendix 4.

Appendix 1: Search strategy

The specialist library at the NSPCC was used initially as it holds many of the relevant journals, books and resources and can access other library catalogues and use inter-library loans. This uncovered much of the relevant research literature. Further searches were then undertaken using bibliographic databases and library catalogues. The databases of research funding bodies were then searched for relevant material and specific organisations working in the area were targeted. The internet was used to search websites and catalogues and was useful for accessing overseas material. Contact was made with researchers working within the field to try to ensure relevant material was included.

The search strategy for the literature review included the use of:

- NSPCC library and Inform website
- bibliographic databases, such as Caredata, ChildData, ENB Health Care Database, PubMed (MEDLINE and Pre-MEDLINE), Social Policy Virtual Library, National Clearinghouse on Child Abuse & Neglect Information database
- library catalogue searches of the British Library, COPAC (covers 21 of largest university libraries in the UK), Electronic Library for Health, Electronic Library for Social Care, British Medical Association Library Catalogue, Royal Society of Medicine Catalogue, Royal College of Nursing Library Catalogue
- databases of research bodies (current and completed research), such as the JRF Knowledgebase, Regard – ESRC, National Research Register – NHS, ReFeR – DoH research findings register, POINT – DoH, Home Office research, TRIP – turning research into practice, Children's Bureau Express
- contact with international and national research networks (Childhood, ChildProtect, Research in Practice)
- contact with organisations known to undertake research in the area (to ensure coverage of current research). For example, universities (via Braintrack Universities Index), National Children's Bureau, Research in Practice, VOLNET

> UK (Barnardo's, National Youth Agency, Community Development Fund, Volunteer Centre), Centre for Research on Families and Relationships, Institute for Public Policy Research, Scottish Office, Welsh Office

■ search of the grey literature, unpublished and internal papers and reports.

Searching databases was complicated because of the range of types of adversity that were covered in the review and because the review was specifically aiming to find research in which children had participated directly. This meant that a whole range of different search terms were used and combined depending on the database.

Examples of search terms included: substance abuse/misuse, alcohol abuse/misuse, drug abuse/misuse, solvent abuse/misuse, parent/s/ing, children of addicted parents, parental illness, mentally ill parents, children's attitudes, children of alcoholic parents, children in violent families, runaway children, runaway youth, drug/s, child/abuse, user views, violence in the home, disabled people/parents, sick people/parents, mental/physical health, children's views, domestic violence, child/ren, violence, children of impaired parents.

Appendix 2: Limitations of the research

Research undertaken with children on their experiences of domestic violence, parental substance misuse and parental ill health is largely qualitative. Qualitative research methods are more often used in this field because they allow for collection of in-depth contextual information about children and families that can enhance our understanding of situations, feelings and behaviours. Qualitative methods also allow more flexibility which can be particularly useful when undertaking research with children. Quantitative methods have been used in more general surveys to children about their families and their understanding of parental problems, such as domestic violence and in surveys to young adults about retrospective childhood experiences (Gilvarry,1994; Cawson and others, 2000).

Undertaking research with children whose parents are in or have been through difficult times is challenging. One of the biggest limitations to research in this area is that children whose parents have experienced domestic violence, substance misuse or ill health have usually been contacted via existing services. A few studies have tried advertising for research participants but this has often met with limited success (Laybourn and others, 1996). The result, however, is that it is difficult to know the potential impact of the views of children that are not accessed and to what extent their experiences are similar to those of children that have been in contact with services.

Sampling via statutory or voluntary agencies also means that professionals can potentially influence which families are approached. Professionals (often with good reason) may believe that a researcher making an approach is not in the best interests of the family or in some cases they may wish to protect their own practice if they feel under threat. This may impact upon the sample, in that less chaotic families may be those approached or those that feel able to come forward. Parents and children may also be reluctant to give consent to take part in research, particularly if they fear intervention by statutory agencies or, in the case of parents, they have concerns about the affect that talking about difficult times may have on their children.

For these reasons it is easier to approach children over 18 and ask them to reflect on their childhood experiences, although this method is clearly reliant on respondents' memories. Another approach is to analyse information provided by children to helplines, however this may not be recorded accurately or information may be incomplete.

The nature of the difficulties in accessing children to be involved in studies may compromise desirable attributes in sample structure. For example Aldridge and Becker (2003), who completed a study of 40 families caring for parents with a mental illness, found that their original intention to stratify their sample by gender, age, race, diagnostic category and whom the young people cared for was not realistically possible. Studies also frequently report not recruiting as many families as originally hoped for.

Research so far that has been undertaken directly with children rarely reflects a long-term perspective. Most of the studies included in this review have only interviewed children at one point in time, providing a useful snapshot but not necessarily capturing children's experiences, feelings and coping mechanisms over a longer period.

A couple of studies reviewed have included a control group. This can be helpful in order to explore the extent to which experiences of children can be attributed solely to the parental problem, for example substance misuse, or to broader individual, family or environmental factors. Concerns about the attribution of problems have been raised, particularly in the field of parental ill health research where early studies were not necessarily seeing children's role in these families within a wider context of socio-economically disadvantaged families and communities.

Appendix 3: Completed studies that include children's perspectives and adults' retrospective accounts

Key reference	Place (if known)	Number and age of children (if known)	Sample recruitment	Method
Laybourn, A, Brown, J and Hill, M (1996) *Hurting on the inside: children's experiences of parental alcohol misuse.* Avebury	Scotland	20 children (aged 5–28 years) from 14 families and their parents	families were recruited via a range of different agencies	interviews
Brisby, T, Baker, S and Hedderwick, T (1997) *Under the influence: coping with parents who drink too much.* Alcohol Concern	UK	3 children (aged 11–14)	no information is given about how they were identified	interviews
Christensen, E (1997) Aspects of a preventative approach to support children of alcoholics, *Child Abuse Review*, 6, 24–34	Denmark	32 children (between 5 and 16 years old) from 20 families and their parents	families were recruited via an alcohol treatment centre	interviews
Houston, A, Kork, S and McLeod, M (1997) *Beyond the limit: children who live with parental alcohol misuse.* ChildLine	UK	studied 3,255 records from ChildLine (2,134 in depth) in which children spoke about parental alcohol problems	ChildLine	calls to the helpline

Malpique, C and others (1998) Violence and alcoholism in the family: how are the children affected? *Alcohol and alcoholism*, 33, 1, 42–6	Portugal	20 families with 21 children	families of in-patients and out-patients attending a Child and Adolescent Psychiatry Department	interviews and psychological tests
Murray, B L (1998) Perceptions of adolescents living with parental alcoholism, *Journal of Psychiatric and Mental Health Nursing*, 5, 525–34	Canada	5 adolescents (aged 13–19 years old)	identified via Al-Anon, informal contacts and a local school	interviews
Gilvarry, C M (1994) *National Association of Children of Alcoholics quantification study: Is there really a problem?* NACOA	UK	1,006 adults (aged 18 or over)	nationally representative sample from telephone lists	telephone survey
Velleman, R and Orford, J (1999) *Risk and resilience: adults who were the children of problem drinkers*. Harwood Academic Publishers	UK	164 adults (16–35 years old) and a comparison group of 80 adults whose parents were not problem drinkers	identified via advertising, personal contacts and statutory/voluntary sector groups	two interviews with each adult undertaken with a gap of 12 months
Liverpool Drug and Alcohol Action Team (2001) *In a different world*. Liverpool DAAT and Barnardo's	UK	25 parents and 20 children	identified via drug misuse teams	group and individual interviews with children using an imaginary family scenario
Barnard, M A and Barlow, J (2003) Discovering parental drug dependence: silence and disclosure, *Children and Society*, 17, 45–56	Scotland	62 parents and 36 children and young people (aged 8–22 years old). Of which 23 were resident with the drug dependent parent	in-treatment and out-of-treatment parents were interviewed. Children and young people identified via parents	interviews and focus groups

Templeton, L and others (2003) *Evaluation of the pilot Family Alcohol Service: final report.* Report to the Camelot Foundation, June 2003	London	11 children from seven families	identified via Family Alcohol Service	interviews

Domestic violence

Ericksen, J R and Henderson, A D (1992) Witnessing family violence: the children's experience, *Journal of Advanced Nursing*, 17, 1200–1209	Canada	13 children (aged between 4 and 12 years)	identified via temporary independent housing	interviews
Abrahams, C (1994) *The hidden victims – children and domestic violence*. NCH Action for Children	UK	questionnaires were completed by 108 women who had 246 children. Follow-up interviews were completed with 15 mothers and 7 children	NCH family centres	questions and interviews
Saunders, A with Epstein, C, Keep, G and Debbonaire, T (1995) *It hurts me too: children's experiences of domestic violence and refuge life.* WAFE/Childline/NISW	UK	5 adults' retrospective experiences and 126 children (aged 11–15) that called ChildLine over a six-month period and mentioned domestic violence	ChildLine	case studies and helpline calls
Hendessi, M (1997) *Voices of children witnessing domestic violence: a form of child abuse.* Coventry City Council Domestic Violence Focus Group	Coventry	22 children and young people (17 aged under 17)	children were living in refuges or in the community	individual or group interviews

Cawson, P and others (2000) *Child maltreatment in the United Kingdom.* NSPCC and Cawson, P (2002) *Child maltreatment in the family*, NSPCC	UK	2,869 young people aged 18–24	random probability sample using a postcode address file	interviews with Computer Assisted Personal Interviewing
McGee, C (2000) *Childhood experiences of domestic violence.* Jessica Kingsley Publishers	Britain	54 children (aged 5–17); two young adults aged 19 and 24; and 48 mothers	recruited via mail-outs to relevant organisations, direct media publicity, approaches from workers from statutory and voluntary agencies	interviews
Mullender and others (2002) *Children's perspectives on domestic violence.* Sage	England	Questionnaire to 1,395 children aged 8–16 in schools. Interviews with 45 children who had lived with DV (and a further 9 children in groups). 3 sub-samples of children (2 of diverse ethnicity and 1 black) were tracked from recruitment to the end of the study (18 months). There were 22 interviews with mothers and 14 with workers	accessed via schools, inter-agency DV forums, Women's Aid groups, women's support group, etc.	questionnaire to school group and interviews with children

Parental physical or mental health problems

Grimshaw, R (1991) *Children of parents with Parkinson's disease: A research report for the Parkinson's Disease Society*. National Children's Bureau	UK		via hospital services and the Parkinson's Disease Society	case studies and survey of people in contact with charity

Bilsborrow, S (1992) *'You grow up fast as well ...': young carers on Merseyside.* Carers National Association, Personal Services Society and Barnardo's	England	11 young people (aged 9–21 years). Includes 2 ex-carers	via service providers	interviews
Elliot, A (1992) *Hidden children: a study of ex-young carers of parents with mental health problems in Leeds.* Leeds City Council: Department of Social Services	Leeds, England	interviews with 9 ex-young carers	identified via parents attending a psychiatric day centre plus personal contacts	interviews
Aldridge, J and Becker, S (1993) *Children who care: inside the world of young carers,* Loughborough University: Young Carers Research Group	Nottingham, England	11 case studies of children (aged 3–18) and 4 former carers	identified via contact with professionals. Self-selection tried via radio but unsuccessful	each person was interviewed twice
Dearden, C and Becker, S (1995) *Young carers: the facts.* Reed Business Publishing	UK	survey of over 600 young carers, case studies with 8 children aged 8–20 years	accessed through young carers projects	survey and case studies
Frank, J (1995) *Couldn't care more: a study of young carers and their needs.* The Children's Society	Hampshire, England	16 young people providing care for a parent/grandparent/ sibling were interviewed. A few former carers and parents were also interviewed	statutory and voluntary agencies and schools	interviews
Dearden, C and Becker, S (1996) *Young carers at the crossroads: an evaluation of the Nottingham Young Carers Project*	Nottingham, England	number of children not given	identified via young carers service	interviews

Newton, B and Becker, S (1996) *Young carers in Southwark: the hidden face of community care*, Loughborough University	London, England	11 case studies of children (aged 3–18) and 4 former young carers	identified via services and organisations in the borough	interviews
Walker, A (1996) *Young carers and their families. A* survey carried out by the Social Division of the Office for National Statistics on behalf of the Department of Health	UK	14 young people (aged 8–17)	via general population sample	interviews
Garley, D and others (1997) Children of the mentally ill: a qualitative focus group approach, *Journal of Psychiatric Mental Health Nursing, 4, 2, 97–103*	Canada	6 children aged 11–15 years old	via an outpatient clinic of university affiliated psychiatric facility	focus groups
Booth, T and Booth, W (1998) *Exceptional childhoods, unexceptional children: growing up with parents who have learning difficulties.* Family Policy Studies Centre in association with the Joseph Rowntree Foundation	UK	30 now-adult children (16 men and 14 women with a median age of 27)	via services	interviews
Centre for the Child and Society and Strathclyde Centre for Disability Research (1999) *Children affected by the disability of another family member: report submitted to Renfrewshire Council.* University of Glasgow	Scotland	interviews with 18 service providers, postal survey of parents/carers (68 respondents) and interviews with 21 children	accessed via range of professionals	interviews

Frank, J, Tatum, C and Tucker, S (1999) *On small shoulders: learning from the experiences of former young carers*, The Children's Society	Hampshire, England	25 interviews, 41 questionnaires	advertising and network of carers	interviews and telephone questions and three case studies
Shah, R and Hatton, C (1999) *Caring alone: young carers in South Asian communities*. Barnardo's	UK	interviews with 19 young carers (aged 8–20 years old) in 13 households	identified via two young carers projects	interviews and focus groups
Strathclyde Centre for Disability Research and Centre for the Child and Society (1999) *The extent, nature and needs of young carers in Easterhouse: report submitted to Greater Glasgow Health Board and Easterhouse Carers Strategy group*. University of Glasgow	Scotland	school survey with 509 respondents (pupils aged 11–17); survey with 20 parents/carers; and two focus groups (with 12 young carers and 12 non young-carers); interviews with 14 young carers	accessed via range of professionals	focus groups and interviews
Bibby, A and Becker, S eds (2000) *Young carers in their own words*. Calouste Gulbenkian Foundation	UK	30 young carers (aged between 9 and 18)	they were accessed through young carers projects	accounts and structured conversations
Dearden, C and Becker, S (2000) *Growing up caring: vulnerability and transition to adulthood – young carers' experiences*. Published by the Youth Work Press for the Joseph Rowntree Foundation	UK	60 young people (aged 16–25)	young people were identified via existing support services for carers	interviews

Jones, A, Jeyasingham, D and Rajasooriya, S (2002) *Invisible families: the strengths and needs of black families in which young people have caring responsibilities*. Policy Press	UK	consultation events with 13 young people; training of 3 'young carers' as peer researchers; interviews with 17 young people and 15 family members from 20 families	centre for young people in Manchester	consultation events, research training and interviews
University of Stirling (2002) *'We all just work together': young people's perspectives of caring in the rural Stirling area*. University of Stirling for the Princess Royal Trust Stirling Carers Centre	Stirling, Scotland	310 young people completed a survey. 6 young people (aged between 10 and 17) were interviewed	survey via three schools	postal questionnaire and interviews
Aldridge, J and Becker, S (2003) *Children who care for parents with mental illness: the perspectives of young carers, parents and professionals*. Policy Press	UK	40 families (children and parents) and 40 key workers in first round of interviews, 28 families and 9 professionals in the second round	young carers projects and National Schizophrenia Fellowship (now named Rethink) projects	interviews on two occasions with ten months in between
Stallard, P and others (in press) *The effects of parental mental illness upon children: a descriptive study of the views of parents and children*. Clinical Child Psychology and Psychiatry	England	24 adults and 26 children from 16 families (aged 6–17 years old)	the adults were attending a community mental health team	interviews
Olsen, R and Clarke, H (2003) *Parenting and disability: disabled parents' experiences of raising children*. Policy Press	UK	80 families with one or two disabled parents, 60 children	via voluntary and statutory services	interviews

Appendix 4: Ongoing studies that include children's perspectives and adults' retrospective accounts

Reference	Focus of study	Sample and methods
Bancroft, A., Experiences of older children of drug- and alcohol-using parents: risk and resilience. Edinburgh University	Parental alcohol and drug misuse	Sample will consist of 40 young people, 20 men and 20 women between the ages of 16–19 who have or had at least one substance-misusing parent. The sample will be varied and recruited using a variety of methods
Cleaver, H., What works? The response of child protection practices and procedures to children exposed to domestic violence or drug and alcohol abuse within their families. Royal Holloway, University of London	Domestic violence and parental substance misuse (alcohol and drugs)	Study of 30 councils and policy documents in agencies represented on the Area Child Protection Committee. Postal questionnaire to senior/ first-line managers/trainers. 360 social work files (from six authorities) will explore how referrals are dealt with in councils with different working practices. Qualitative sample of 42 cases (7 from each of the six councils). Interviews will be carried out with young people, parents, and relevant professionals
Cogan, N., Children affected by mental health problems in the family. PhD thesis, Glasgow University	Parental health problems (physical or mental)	Interviews with 20 children (aged 12–17years) whose parent/s experience mental health problems, their parents and key informants. They will be identified via the mental health team. A control group of parents and children will also be used
Gruenert, S. Zavrou, N. Ratnam, S. and Marks, M., Nobody's Client Project. Victoria, Australia	Parental alcohol and drug misuse	Action research project that aims to work with a hundred 5–12 year olds whose parents have drug- and alcohol-related problems, and who are currently receiving drug treatment. The project aims to interview children directly, as well as their parents or carers and their teachers

Kearney, J. and Taylor, N., Report of the first stage (interviews with parents): Kearney, J. and Taylor, N. The highs and lows of family life: report of a two-year research project. Bolton Home-Start/Institute for Public Health Research and Policy (IPHRP) University of Salford	Parental alcohol misuse	42 drug-using parents, carers and a partner of a drug-using parent were interviewed. A focus group and two case studies were also completed. 'Snowballing' was used via informal contacts, contact with parents and carers via services, drop-ins, peer networks. Children to be interviewed in the second stage of this project.
Manby, M., Children of drug and alcohol users – experiences of care and support. Nationwide Children's Research Centre	Parental alcohol and drug misuse	Interviews to be undertaken with 20 young carers/young users of counselling services

References

Abrahams, C (1994) *The hidden victims: children and domestic violence.* NCH Action for Children

Advisory Council on the Misuse of Drugs (2003) *Hidden harm: Responding to the needs of children of problem drug users.* Home Office www.drugs.gov.uk

Aldgate, J and Statham, J (2001) *The Children Act now: messages from research.* Department of Health

Aldridge, J and Becker, S (1993) *Children who care: inside the world of young carers.* Loughborough University: Young Carers Research Group

Aldridge, J and Becker, S (2003) *Children who care for parents with mental illness: the perspectives of young carers, parents and professionals.* Policy Press

Baginsky, M ed. (2001) *Counselling and support services for young people aged 12–16 who have experienced sexual abuse.* NSPCC

Bancroft, A and others (2002) *Support for the families of drug-users: a review of the literature.* Centre for Research on Families and Relationships, University of Edinburgh and Scottish Executive, Drug Misuse Research Programme

Banks, P and others (2001) 'Seeing the invisible children and young people affected by disability', *Disability and Society,* 16, 6, 797–814

Banks, P and others of the Scottish Executive Central Research Unit (2002) *Young carers: assessments and services: literature review of identification, needs assessment and service provision for young carers and their families.* The Stationery Office (Edinburgh)

Barnard, M A and Barlow, J (2003) 'Discovering parental drug dependence: silence and disclosure', *Children and Society,* 17, 1, 45–56

Bates, T and others (1999) *Drug use, parenting and child protection: Towards an effective interagency response.* University of Central Lancashire

Berridge, D (1997) *Foster care: a research review*. The Stationery Office

Bibby, A and Becker, S eds (2000) *Young carers in their own words*. Calouste Gulbenkian Foundation

Bilsborrow, S (1992) *'You grow up fast as well...': young carers on Merseyside*. Carers National Association, Personal Services Society and Barnardo's

Booth, T and Booth, W (1998) *Exceptional childhoods, unexceptional children: growing up with parents who have learning difficulties*. Family Policy Studies Centre in association with the Joseph Rowntree Foundation

Brandon, M and others (1999) *Safeguarding children with the Children Act 1989*. The Stationery Office

Brisby, T, Baker, S and Hedderwick, T (1997) *Under the influence: coping with parents who drink too much*. Alcohol Concern

Bullock, R, Little, M and Millham, S (1993) *Residential care for children: a review of the research*. The Stationery Office

Burman, M, Brown, J and Batchelor, S '"Taking it to heart": girls and the meanings of violence' *in* Stanko, B ed. (2003) *The meanings of violence*. Routledge

Butler, I and Williamson, H (1994) *Children speak: children, trauma and social work*. Longman

Cawson, P and others (2000) *Child maltreatment in the United Kingdom*. NSPCC

Cawson, P (2002) *Child maltreatment in the family*. NSPCC

Centre for the Child and Society and Strathclyde Centre for Disability Research (1999) *Children affected by the disability of another family member: Report submitted to Renfrewshire Council*. University of Glasgow

ChildLine (1995) *What children tell ChildLine about being abused*. ChildLine

ChildLine (1998) *Unhappy families, unhappy children*. ChildLine

Christensen, E (1997) 'Aspects of a preventative approach to support children of alcoholics' *Child Abuse Review*, 6, 24–34

Cleaver, H, Unell, I and Aldgate, J (1999) *Children's needs – Parenting capacity: The impact of parental mental illness, problem alcohol and drug use and domestic violence on children's development*. The Stationery Office

Corby, B (2000) *Child abuse: towards a knowledge base.* Open University

Cowling, V ed. (1999) *Children of parents with mental illness.* Australia, Victoria: The Australian Council for Educational Research

Dearden, C and Becker, S (1995) *Young carers: the facts.* Reed Business Publishing

Dearden, C and Becker, S (1996) *Young carers at the crossroads: an evaluation of the Nottingham Young Carers Project*

Dearden, C and Becker, S (1998) 'The needs and experiences of young carers in the UK' *Childright*, 148, 15–16

Dearden, C and Becker, S (2000) *Growing up caring: vulnerability and transition to adulthood – young carers' experiences.* Published by the Youth Work Press for the Joseph Rowntree Foundation

Department for Education and Skills (2003a) *Every Child Matters.* The Stationery Office

Department for Education and Skills (2003b) *Statistics of Education: Referrals, Assessments and Children and Young People on the Child Protection Registers, Year Ending 31 March 2003.* The Stationery Office

Department of Health (1995) *Child protection: messages from research.* HMSO

Department of Health (2003a) *Getting the Right Start: The National Service Framework for Children, Young People and Maternity Services - Emerging Findings* http://www.dh.gov.uk/assetRoot/04/07/53/37/04075337.pdf

Department of Health (2003b) *Women's mental health: into the mainstream. Strategic development of mental health care for women*

Domestic Violence Advice Line (1997) *"Safe to talk": (Voices from the Refuge). An interim report on the effects of domestic violence on children living in Gloucestershire*

Drug Strategy Directorate (2002) *Updated Drug Strategy.* Home Office

Dunn, J and Deater-Deckard, K (2001) *Children's views of their changing families.* Joseph Rowntree Foundation

Elliott, A (1992) *Hidden children: a study of ex-young carers of parents with mental health problems in Leeds.* Mental Health Development Section, Department of Social Services: Leeds City Council

Ericksen, J R and Henderson, A D (1992) 'Witnessing family violence: the children's experience', *Journal of Advanced Nursing*, 17, 1200–9

Falkov, A (1996) *Study of working together 'part 8' reports: fatal child abuse and parenting psychiatric disorder.* Department of Health

Farmer, E and Owen, M (1995) *Child protection practice: private risks and public remedies.* HMSO

Forrester, D (2000) 'Parental substance misuse and child protection in a British sample: A survey of children on the Child Protection Register in an inner London district office', *Child Abuse Review,* 9, 4

Forrester, D (2002) 'Picking up the pieces', *Community Care,* 12–18 December, 36–7

Frank, J (1995) *Couldn't care more: a study of young carers and their needs.* The Children's Society

Frank, J, Tatum, C and Tucker, S (1999) *On small shoulders: Learning from the experiences of former young carers.* The Children's Society

Fraser, M ed. (1997) *Risk and resilience in childhood.* US, Washington: NASW

Frosh, S and Phoenix, A (1999) *Emergent identities: masculinity and 11–14-year-old boys.* ESRC Children 5 to 16 Programme, Hull University

Fuller, R and others (2000) *Young people and welfare: Negotiating pathways.* University of Stirling: ESRC

Gardner, R (2003) *Supporting families: child protection in the community.* Wiley

Garley, D and others (1997) 'Children of the mentally ill: a qualitative focus group approach', *Journal of Psychiatric Mental Health Nursing,* 4, 2, 97–103

Ghate, D and Daniels, A (1997) *Talking about my generation.* NSPCC

Ghate, D and Hazel, N (2002) *Parenting in poor environments: stress, coping and support.* Jessica Kingsley

Gilligan, R (2000) 'Adversity, resilience and young people: The protective value of positive school and spare time experiences' *Children and Society,* 14, 1, 37–47

Gilvarry, C M (1994) *National Association of Children of Alcoholics quantification study: Is there really a problem?* NACOA

Gorin, S (forthcoming) *A pilot study of child protection, family characteristics and physical punishment: briefing.* NSPCC

Grimshaw, R (1991) *Children of parents with Parkinson's disease: A research report for the Parkinson's Disease Society.* National Children's Bureau

Grotberg, E 'The International Resilience Project' *in* John, M *ed.* (1997) *A charge against society: the child's right to protection.* Jessica Kingsley

Hague, G and others with Debbonaire, T (1996) *Children, domestic violence and refuges: a study of needs and responses.* Women's Aid Federation (England)

Harbin, F and Murphy, M (2000) *Substance misuse and child care: how to understand, assist and intervene when drugs affect parenting.* Russell House Publishing

Hawthorne, J and others (2003) *Supporting children through family change: a review of interventions and services for children of divorcing and separating parents.* YPS Family Change series. Joseph Rowntree Foundation

Hester, M, Pearson, C and Harwin, N (1998) *Making an impact: children and domestic violence.* Barnardo's; School for Policy Studies; University of Bristol; NSPCC; Department of Health. Barnardo's

Hey, V (1997) *The company she keeps: an ethnography of girls' friendships.* Open University Press

Hill, M (1999) 'What's the problem? Who can help? The perspectives of children and young people on their well-being and on helping professionals', *Journal of Social Work Practice*, 13, 2, 136–45

Hill, M, Laybourn, A and Brown, J (1996) 'Children whose parents misuse alcohol – a study of services and needs', *Child and Family Social Work*, 1, 159–67

Hindle, D (1998) 'Growing up with a parent who has a chronic mental illness: one child's perspective', *Child and Family Social Work*, 3, 259–66

Hogan, D (1998) 'Annotation: The psychological development and welfare of children of opiate and cocaine users: review and research needs', *Journal of Child Psychology and Psychiatry*, 39, 5, 609–20

Hogan, D and Higgins, L (2001) *When parents use drugs? Key findings from a study of children in the care of drug-using parents.* Children's Research Centre, Trinity College Dublin

Home Office (2003) *Safety and justice: the Government's proposals on domestic violence* http://www.homeoffice.gov.uk/docs2/violence.html

Home Office Advisory Council for the Misuse of Drugs (2003) *Hidden harm – responding to the needs of children of problem drug users* http://www.homeoffice.gov.uk/docs2/hiddenharm.pdf

Houston, A, Kork, S and McLeod, M (1997) *Beyond the limit: children who live with parental alcohol misuse.* ChildLine

Humphreys, C (2001) *The impact of domestic violence on children.* Open University Press

Humphreys, C and Mullender, A (2000) *Children and domestic violence: a research overview of the impact on children.* Research in Practice

Jaffe, P G, Wolfe, D A and Wilson, S K (1990) *Children of battered women.* US, Newbury Park, California: Sage

Jones, A, Jeyasingham, D and Rajasooriya, S (2002) *Invisible families: the strengths and needs of black families in which young people have caring responsibilities.* Policy Press

Kearney, J and Taylor, N (2001) *The highs and lows of family life: report of a two-year research project.* Bolton Home-Start/Institute for Public Health Research and Policy, University of Salford

Kroll, B and Taylor, A (2003) *Parental substance misuse and child welfare.* Jessica Kingsley

Landells, S and Pritlove, J (1994) *Young carers of a parent with schizophrenia: a Leeds survey.* Department of Social Services, Leeds

Laybourn, A, Brown, J and Hill, M (1996) *Hurting on the inside: children's experiences of parental alcohol misuse.* Avebury

Liverpool Drug and Alcohol Action Team (2001) *In a different world.* Liverpool Drug and Alcohol Action Team and Barnardo's

Livingston, J (1998) *Alcohol and motherhood: a qualitative study of the experiences of eight young women whose mothers have an alcohol problem.* MSc dissertation, Robert Gordon University

McGee, C (2000) *Childhood experiences of domestic violence.* Jessica Kingsley

McKeganey, N, Barnard, M and McIntosh, J (2002) 'Paying the price for their parents' drug use: the impact of parental drug use on children', *Drug Education, Prevention and Policy,* 3, 233–46

MacLeod, M (1996) *Talking with children about child abuse: ChildLine's first ten years.* ChildLine

MacLeod, M and Barter, C (1996) *We know it's tough to talk: boys in need of help.* ChildLine

Malpique, C and others (1998) 'Violence and alcoholism in the family: how are the children affected?' *Alcohol and alcoholism,* 33, 1, 42–6

Marlowe, J (1996) 'Helpers, helplessness and self-help: "Shaping the silence", a personal account' *in* Gopfert, M, Webster, J and Seeman, M V eds *Parental psychiatric disorder, distressed parents and their families.* Cambridge University Press

Mirrlees-Black, C (1999) *Domestic violence: findings from a new British crime survey self-completion questionnaire.* Home Office Research Study No. 191. Home Office

Mooney, J (1994) *The hidden figure: domestic violence in North London.* London Borough of Islington, Police and Crime Prevention Unit/Middlesex University, Centre for Criminology

Morrow, V (1998) *Understanding families: children's perspectives.* National Children's Bureau in association with Joseph Rowntree Foundation

Mullender, A and Morley, R (1994) *Children living with domestic violence: putting men's abuse of women on the child care agenda.* Whitting and Birch

Mullender, A and others (2002) *Children's perspectives on domestic violence.* Sage

Murray, B L (1998) 'Perceptions of adolescents living with parental alcoholism', *Journal of Psychiatric and Mental Health Nursing,* 5, 525–34

Newman, T (2002) '"Young carers" and disabled parents: time for a change of direction?' *Disability and Society,* 17, 6, 613–25

Newton, B and Becker, S (1996) *Young carers in Southwark: The hidden face of community care.* Loughborough University

Olsen, R (1996) 'Young carers: challenging the facts and politics of research into children and caring', *Disability and Society,* 11, 41–54

Olsen, R and Clarke, H (2003) *Parenting and disability: disabled parents' experiences of raising children.* Policy Press

Olsen, R and Parker, G (1997) 'A response to Aldridge and Becker, "Disability rights and the denial of young carers: the dangers of zero-sum arguments"', *Critical Social Policy,* 50, 17, 125–33

Orford, J (2001) *Excessive appetites: a psychological view of addictions.* 2nd edn, John Wiley

Osbourne, D (2001) 'Abused young people's views of adult intervention: an Irish study', *Social Work in Europe,* 8, 1, 11–21

Parton, N and Wattam, C eds (1999) *Child sexual abuse: responding to the experiences of children.* John Wiley and Sons

Prime Minister's Strategy Unit (2004) *Alcohol Harm Reduction Strategy for England.* http://www.strategy.gov.uk/output/page3669.asp

Quinton, D and Rutter, M (19 & 5) 'Family pathology and child psychiatric disorder: a four year prospective study', *in* Nicol, A R ed. *Longitudinal studies in child psychology and psychiatry.* John Wiley and Sons

Saunders, A, with Epstein, C, Keep, G and Debbonaire, T (1995) *It hurts me too: children's experiences of domestic violence and refuge life.* WAFE/Childline/NISW

Scottish Executive (2001) *Getting our priorities right: Policy and practice guidelines for working with children and families affected by problem drug use* http://www.scotland.gov.uk/publications/search.aspx?key=priorities

Scottish Executive (2003) Young runaways and children abused through prostitution. *Working Group Consultation Paper* http://www.scotland.gov.uk/library5/justice/vcyr-02.asp

Segal, J and Simms, J (1993) *My mum needs me: helping children with ill or disabled parents.* Penguin

Shah, R and Hatton, C (1999) *Caring alone: young carers in South Asian communities.* Barnardo's

Social Exclusion Unit (2002) *Young runaways.* Social Exclusion Unit

Stallard, P and others (2004) *The effects of parental mental illness upon children: a descriptive study of the views of parents and children.* Clinical Child Psychology and Psychiatry, 9, 1, 39-52

Strathclyde Centre for Disability Research and Centre for the Child and Society (1999) *The extent, nature and needs of young carers in Easterhouse,* report submitted to Greater Glasgow Health Board and Easterhouse Carers Strategy Group Glasgow: University of Glasgow

Templeton, L and others (2003) *Evaluation of the pilot Family Alcohol Service: final report.* Report to the Camelot Foundation, June 2003

Thoburn, J, Wilding, J and Watson, J (2000) *Family support in cases of emotional maltreatment and neglect.* The Stationery Office

Tunnard, J (2002a) *Parental problem drinking and its impact on children.* Research in Practice

Tunnard, J (2002b) *Parental drug misuse: a review of impact and intervention studies.* Research in Practice

University of Stirling (2002) *'We all just work together': young people's perspectives of caring in the rural Stirling area.* Research briefing. University of Stirling for the Princess Royal Trust Stirling Carers Centre

Velleman, R (1993) *Alcohol and the family.* Occasional Paper, Institute of Alcohol Studies

Velleman, R and Orford, J (1999) *Risk and resilience: adults who were the children of problem drinkers.* Harwood Academic Publishers

Wade, J (2002) *Missing out: young runaways in Scotland.* York University

Walker, A (1996) *Young carers and their families.* A survey carried out by the Social Division of the Office for National Statistics on behalf of the Department of Health

Wates, M and Olsen, R (forthcoming 2003) *Disabled parents: examining research assumptions (Research Review No. 6).* Research in Practice

Wattam, C and Woodward, C (1996) 'And do I abuse my children?...No. 1 – Learning about prevention from people who have experienced child abuse' *in Childhood matters: report of the National Commission of Inquiry into the prevention of child abuse.* (1996) Vol 2: Background papers. The Stationery Office

Webster, A with Coombe, A and Stacey, I (2002) *Bitter legacy: the emotional effects of domestic violence on children.* Barnardo's
www.barnardos.org.uk/resources/researchpublications/documents/BITTRLEG.PDF

Westcott, H (1993) *The abuse of children and adults with disabilities.* NSPCC

Westcott, H and Davies, G (1995) 'Children's help-seeking behaviour', *Child Care Health and Development,* 21, 4, 255–70

Wright, S (2002) *An evaluation of a pilot project to support children and young people affected by domestic violence.* Time4Us, Survivors of Child Abuse, Gloucestershire